RETTA WAREHIME

JACK AND JILL QUILTS

FOR BOYS AND GIRLS

Martingale®
& COMPANY

Jack and Jill Quilts: For Boys and Girls
© 2006 by Retta Warehime

Martingale®
& COMPANY

That Patchwork Place®

That Patchwork Place® is an imprint of Martingale & Company®.

Martingale & Company
20205 144th Avenue NE
Woodinville, WA 98072-8478 USA
www.martingale-pub.com

CREDITS

PRESIDENT: *Nancy J. Martin*
CEO: *Daniel J. Martin*
VP AND GENERAL MANAGER: *Tom Wierzbicki*
PUBLISHER: *Jane Hamada*
EDITORIAL DIRECTOR: *Mary V. Green*
MANAGING EDITOR: *Tina Cook*
TECHNICAL EDITOR: *Laurie Bevan*
COPY EDITOR: *Ellen Balstad*
DESIGN DIRECTOR: *Stan Green*
ILLUSTRATOR: *Robin Strobel*
COVER AND TEXT DESIGNER: *Trina Craig*
PHOTOGRAPHER: *Brent Kane*

MISSION STATEMENT

DEDICATED TO PROVIDING QUALITY
PRODUCTS AND SERVICE
TO INSPIRE CREATIVITY.

Printed in China
11 10 09 08 07 06   8 7 6 5 4 3 2 1

Library of Congress Cataloging-in-Publication Data
Warehime, Retta.
    Jack and Jill quilts : for boys and girls / Retta Warehime.
        p.   cm.
    ISBN 1-56477-645-X
    1. Quilting—Patterns.   2. Patchwork—Patterns.
3. Appliqué—Patterns.   4. Children's quilts.   I. Title.
    TT835.W3566 2006
    746.46'041—dc22

                                        2005022831

DEDICATION

To my friends I loved and lost this past quilting season: my father-in-law, Royal DeBoer, and my quilting friends Terry Tannenburg and Heather Layden.

ACKNOWLEDGMENTS

Thank you to all my friends and family for your generous giving of time, support, and prayers. You are all a blessing!

To my husband, Dan, who always believes in me but has some interesting suggestions when it comes to naming my quilts.

To Catie Senske for sharing her beautiful snow-covered retreat, which is where I wrote this book, and Kathy Renzelman, who drove me there.

To Anne Rettig and Penney Smalley for helping name the quilts, writing descriptions, and sharing all the wonderful lunches—but mostly for the desserts.

To Pam Clarke and Amy Smith for their gorgeous machine quilting and workmanship. I never give direction but always love what they do!

To my beautiful grandchildren, who were my inspiration for this book. Whitney, Cole, Makayla, and Kage—you make me smile!

Through their professionalism and great commitment to the quilting industry, the staff members at Martingale & Company continue to provide new and innovative ideas for us quilters. To everyone there, who works so hard to produce each book, I thank you!

I wish to thank the following fabric companies for providing me with such wonderful fabrics to use in these quilts: Benartex, Inc., Clothworks, Moda Fabrics, and Quilting Treasures. Thanks also to Fairfield Processing Corporation for donating all the batting.

CONTENTS

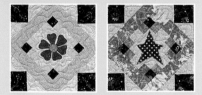

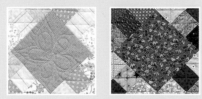

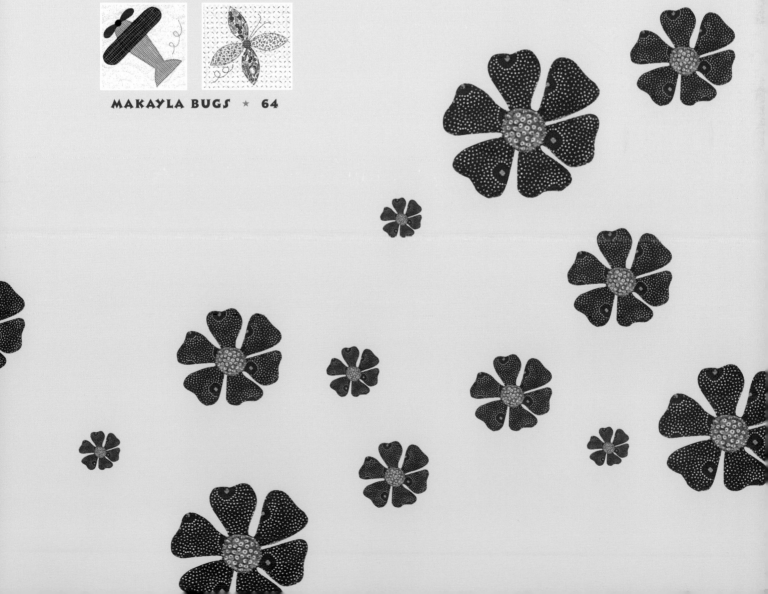

INTRODUCTION

THIS BOOK HAS been an adventure with personal rewards for me. I have found as my children grow older that my thoughts often turn naturally to my grandchildren. They inspire me to look at quilt designs and colors through their eyes—the eyes of children—and this is how I created the projects for this book. As a result, the designs and colors are not in my comfort zone but I am pleased with the finished projects. Taking the step of seeing things as a child would was easier than I thought it would be. I guess a bit of child remains in all of us, regardless of our age.

I also challenged myself to make the same quilt pattern look different by creating boy and girl versions of each quilt. Once again I proved the saying, "All

quilts are different and yet the same." As I write this introduction, I want to encourage all quilters, new and not so new, to step out of their own comfort zones.

In the past 25 years as a quilter, I have had a lot of wonderful people enter my life. I enjoy sharing my quilting experiences. It is both comforting and inspirational. It is not just about the quilting, but about friendships, fun, sharing, and creating.

If this is your first time sewing a quilt, I hope I make your quilting experience a little easier. If you've been at it for years, I hope you'll find a quilt within these pages that will inspire you.

I continue to make quilts for my friends and family, and I love every minute of it. My hope is to inspire you to make quilts for everyone you love!

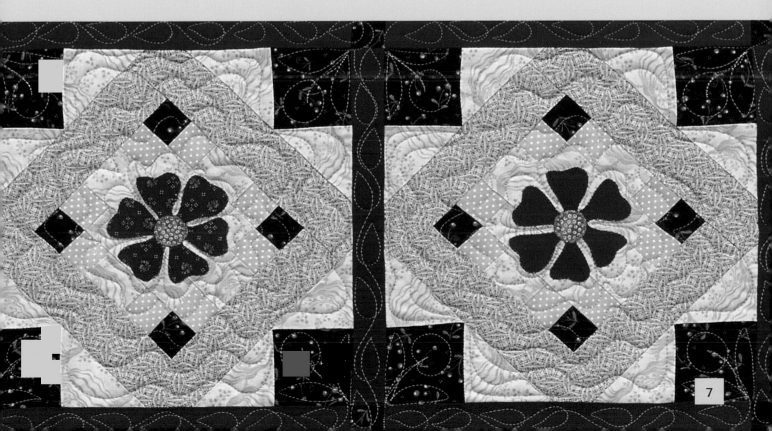

WAHOO! COWBOY

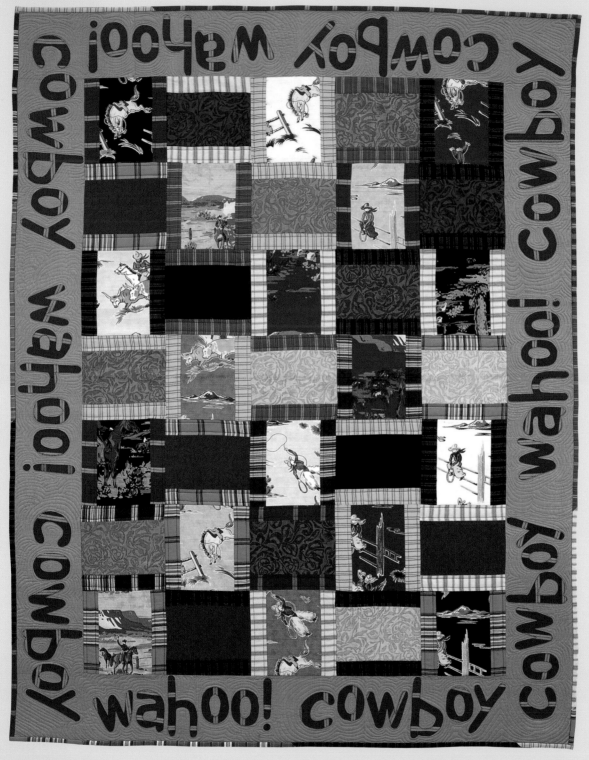

By Retta Warehime

Decorating my friend's cowboy-themed, "Billy the Kid" bunkroom in her Colorado condo inspired me to make this quilt. Squeals of delight are guaranteed when you stitch it up for your favorite cowboy or grown-up cowhand. This quilt was made for Catie Senske.

MATERIALS

All yardages are based on 42"-wide fabric.

* ⅜ yard *each* of 7 print fabrics for vertical rectangles
* ⅜ yard *each* of 7 colors of tone-on-tone fabrics for horizontal rectangles
* ⅜ yard *each* of 7 striped fabrics for sashing strips and binding
* 1⅜ yards of fabric for border
* 1¼ yards of fabric for appliqué letters
* 3½ yards of fabric for backing
* 59" x 75" piece of batting
* 3¼ yards of lightweight fusible web for appliqué

————————— ★ —————————

CUTTING TIPS

When cutting the print rectangles, make sure they are cut so that the design is vertical. And when cutting the striped strips, make sure they are cut so that the stripes run across the width of the strips. Line up the stripe design and cut in pairs if you want each side of the block to match exactly. You may want to cut some extra striped pairs so that you can play with color placement.

—————————————————————

CUTTING

From the striped fabrics, cut a *total* of:
* 35 pairs of strips, 2" x 8½" (70 strips total)
* 2½"-wide binding strips in lengths varying from 12" to 20" (256" total)

From the print fabrics, cut a *total* of:
* 18 rectangles, 5½" x 8½"

From the tone-on-tone fabrics, cut a *total* of:
* 17 rectangles, 5½" x 8½"

From the border fabric, cut:
* 6 strips, 7" x 42"

MAKING THE BLOCKS

Sew the pairs of striped 8½"-long strips to the sides of the print and tone-on-tone rectangles as shown. I did this randomly, but if you're concerned about color placement, you may want to lay out your blocks first. Press the seams toward the strips.

Make 18.

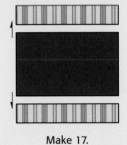
Make 17.

ASSEMBLING THE QUILT TOP

1. Lay out the blocks in seven rows of five blocks each, arranging them until you are happy with the color placement.

2. Sew the blocks into rows, and press the seams in opposite directions from row to row. Join the rows and press all the seams in one direction.

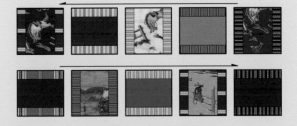

wahoo! cowboy

ADDING THE BORDERS

I used fusible web and machine appliqué to add the letters to this quilt, and this is described in the steps that follow, but feel free to use the method of your choice. Refer to "Appliqué" on page 70 for more detailed instructions.

1. Using the patterns on pages 11–13, prepare the letters for appliqué.

── ★ ──

TRACING TIPS

Trace the curves of the letters first and then use a ruler to trace the straight lines. Doing so makes the tracing process quicker and more accurate.

2. Sew the 7"-wide border strips end to end. From this pieced strip, cut two strips 56½" long for each side border and two strips 53½" long for the top and bottom borders.

3. Lay the border strips along the edges of the quilt and arrange the letters. Fuse all the letters, except those that are in the corners, in place and machine appliqué.

── ★ ──

APPLIQUÉ TIPS

Using a buttonhole stitch, I machine appliquéd the letters to the border strips before they were sewn to the quilt center and fused the letters in the corners after the borders were added. This made it easier to machine appliqué because I only had to handle the whole quilt top for just a few letters.

4. Sew the 56½"-long border strips to the sides of the quilt center and press the seams toward the borders. Sew the 53½"-long strips to the top and bottom and press the seams toward the borders. Be sure the border strips are in the same positions as when you laid them out in step 3. Fuse the remaining letters in the corners and machine appliqué.

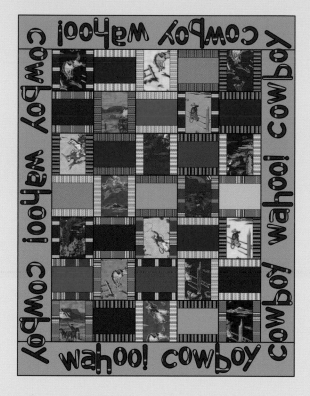

FINISHING THE QUILT

Refer to the quilt finishing techniques on pages 75–79 for more detailed instructions, if needed.

1. Piece the quilt backing so that it's approximately 6" wider and longer than the quilt top. Mark the quilt top if necessary.

2. Layer the quilt top with batting and backing, and baste the layers together. Hand or machine quilt as desired.

3. Trim the batting and backing even with the edges of the quilt top. Add a hanging sleeve if desired. Using the striped 2½"-wide strips, prepare the binding and sew it to the quilt. Make a label and attach it to your quilt.

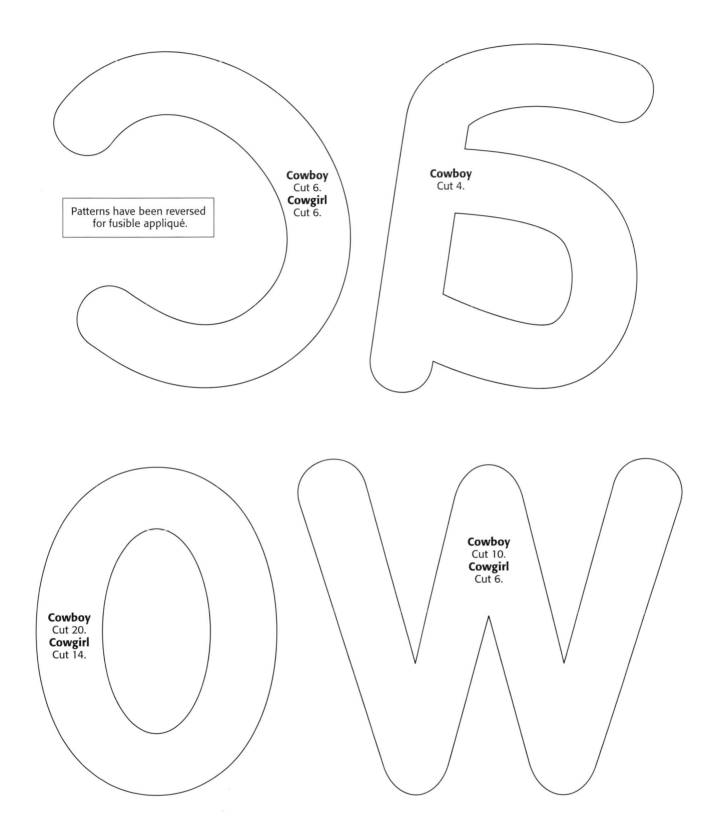

Patterns have been reversed for fusible appliqué.

Cowboy Cut 6. **Cowgirl** Cut 6.

Cowboy Cut 4.

Cowboy Cut 20. **Cowgirl** Cut 14.

Cowboy Cut 10. **Cowgirl** Cut 6.

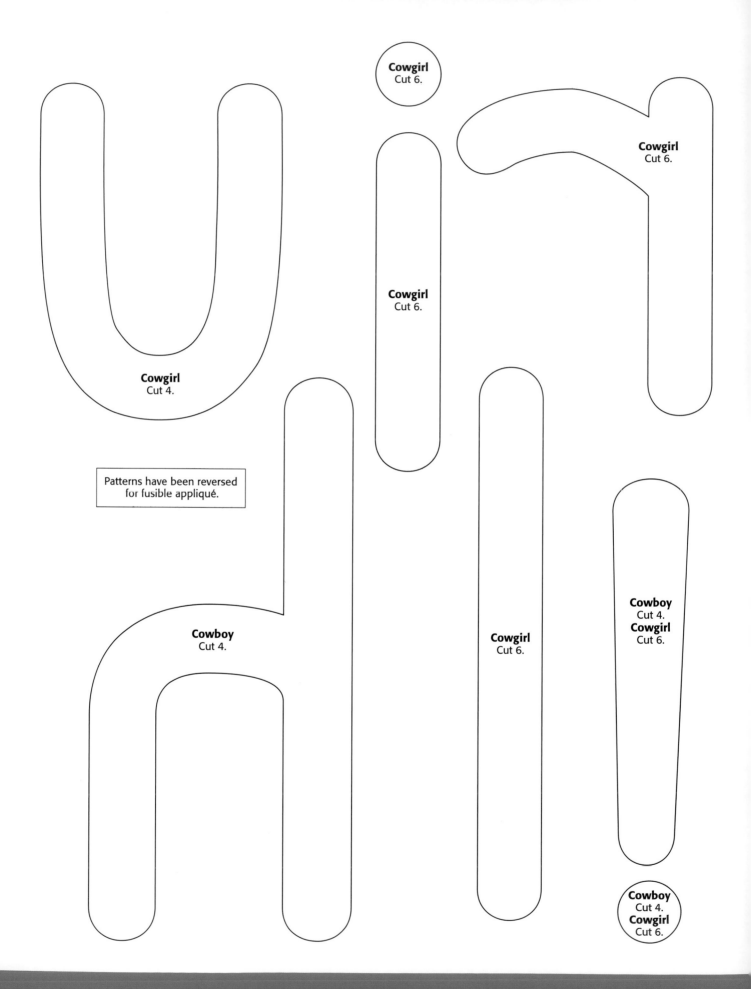

Cowgirl
Cut 6.

Cowgirl
Cut 6.

Cowgirl
Cut 6.

Cowgirl
Cut 4.

Patterns have been reversed
for fusible appliqué.

Cowboy
Cut 4.

Cowgirl
Cut 6.

Cowboy
Cut 4.
Cowgirl
Cut 6.

Cowboy
Cut 4.
Cowgirl
Cut 6.

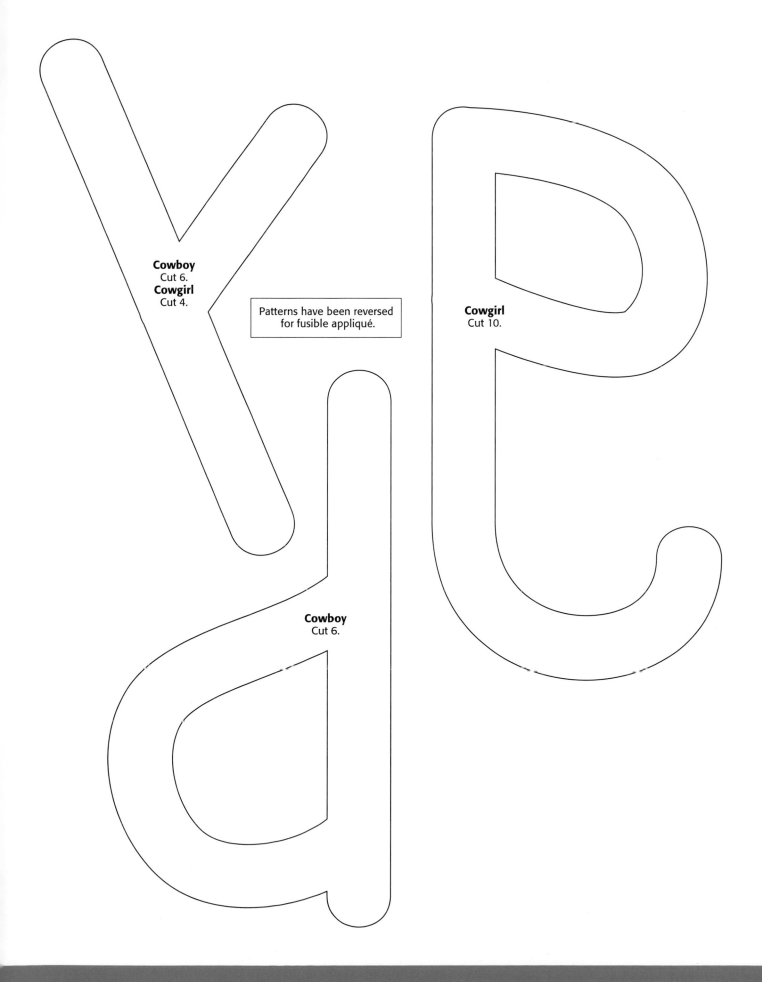

Cowboy
Cut 6.
Cowgirl
Cut 4.

Patterns have been reversed
for fusible appliqué.

Cowgirl
Cut 10.

Cowboy
Cut 6.

YOU GO COWGIRL!

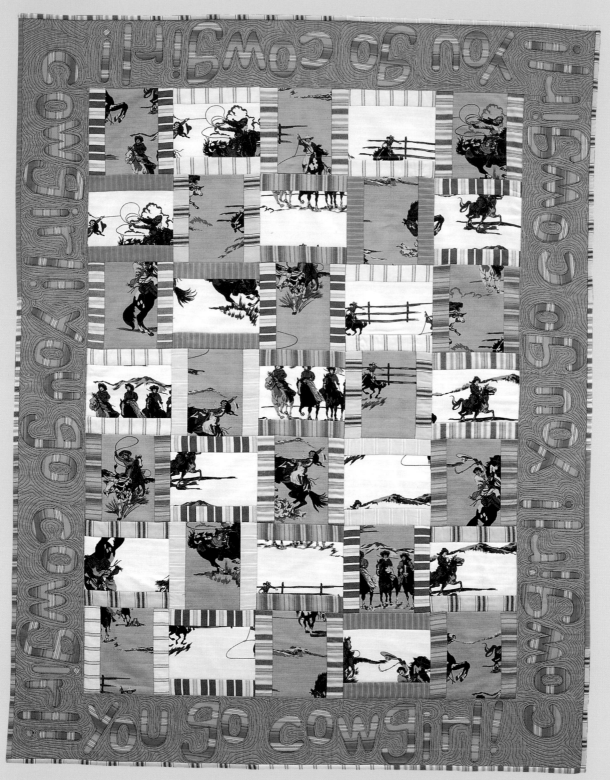

By Retta Warehime
This easily pieced, lap-sized quilt in pink and cream will delight your favorite cowgirl.
I made this version for Whitney Diana Holland, my granddaughter.

Finished Quilt Size: 53" x 69"
Finished Block Size: 8" x 8"

MATERIALS

All yardages are based on 42"-wide fabric.

★ ⅜ yard *each* of 7 striped fabrics for sashing strips and binding
★ 1⅜ yards of fabric for border
★ 1¼ yards of fabric for appliqué letters
★ 1 yard of pink print for vertical rectangles
★ 1 yard of white print for horizontal rectangles
★ 3½ yards of fabric for backing
★ 59" x 75" piece of batting
★ 3¼ yards of lightweight fusible web for appliqué

CUTTING

From the striped fabrics, cut a *total* of:
★ 35 pairs of strips, 2" x 8½" (70 strips total)*
★ 2½"-wide strips in lengths varying from 12" to 20" (256" total)

From the pink print, cut:
★ 18 rectangles, 5½" x 8½" (design should be vertical)

From the white print, cut:
★ 17 rectangles, 5½" x 8½" (design should be horizontal)

From the border fabric, cut:
★ 6 strips, 7" x 42"

See "Cutting Tips" on page 9.

MAKING THE QUILT

Refer to the directions for "Wahoo! Cowboy" beginning on page 9 to assemble this quilt. Note that you will use the white print rectangles in place of the tone-on-tone rectangles, and the pink print rectangles in place of the print rectangles.

CAITLYN'S GARDEN

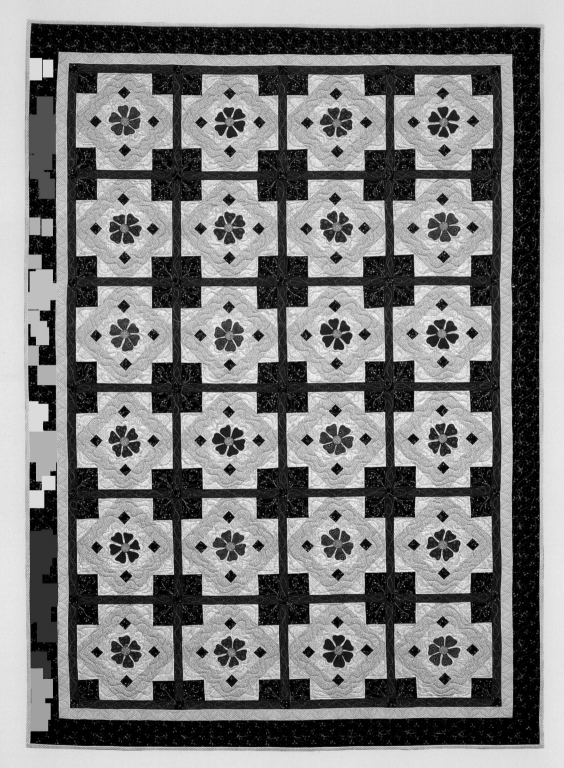

Designed and pieced by Retta Warehime. Machine quilted by Pam Clarke.

While I was designing this special quilt for a young couple who are good friends of our family, the couple's first child was born 10 weeks premature and weighed only 2 pounds, 10 ounces. I decided to dedicate this quilt to their baby instead. Caitlyn Anne Rettig is now an amazingly healthy toddler and the owner of this quilt.

Finished Quilt Size: 57½" x 80½"
Finished Block Size: 10½" x 10½"

MATERIALS

All yardages are based on 42"-wide fabric.

* 2¼ yards of purple print for blocks, cornerstones, and outer border
* 1⅝ yards of cream print for blocks
* 1½ yards of medium tan print for blocks
* 1½ yards of red print for sashing and flowers
* 1⅜ yards of gold print for blocks, inner border, and binding
* ⅛ yard or scrap of green print for flower centers
* 5 yards of fabric for backing
* 64" x 87" piece of batting
* ⅞ yard of lightweight fusible web for appliqué

CUTTING

From the purple print, cut:
* 4 strips, 1½" x 42"
* 9 strips, 3½" x 42"; crosscut into 96 squares, 3½" x 3½"
* 2 strips, 1½" x 42"; crosscut into 35 squares, 1½" x 1½"
* 7 strips, 4½" x 42"

From the gold print, cut:
* 8 strips, 1½" x 42"
* 6 strips, 1¾" x 42"
* 8 strips, 2½" x 42"

From the cream print, cut:
* 2 strips, 2" x 42"
* 2 strips, 4" x 42"
* 4 strips, 2" x 42"; crosscut into 24 rectangles, 2" x 6"
* 9 strips, 3⅜" x 42"; crosscut into 96 squares, 3⅜" x 3⅜". Cut once diagonally to yield 192 triangles.

From the medium tan print, cut:
* 3 strips, 6" x 42"; crosscut into 48 rectangles, 2" x 6"
* 3 strips, 9" x 42"; crosscut into 48 rectangles, 2" x 9"

From the red print, cut:
* 3 strips, 11" x 42"; crosscut into 58 rectangles, 1½" x 11"

MAKING THE BLOCKS

1. Sew two purple 1½"-wide strips, two gold 1½"-wide strips, and one cream 2"-wide strip together to make strip set A. Press the seams toward the cream strip. Repeat to make two strip sets. Cut 48 segments, 1½" wide.

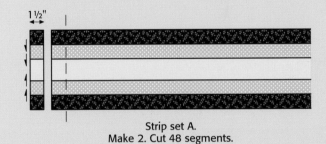

Strip set A.
Make 2. Cut 48 segments.

2. Sew one gold 1½"-wide strip to each side of a cream 4"-wide strip to make strip set B. Press the seams toward the gold strips. Repeat to make two strip sets. Cut 48 segments, 1½" wide.

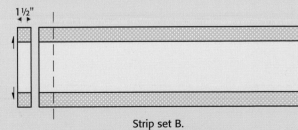

Strip set B.
Make 2. Cut 48 segments.

3. Sew one segment from strip set A and one segment from strip set B together to make 48 A-B units. Press the seams toward segment B.

Make 48.

4. Sew one A-B unit to each side of a cream 2" x 6" rectangle as shown. Press the seams toward the cream rectangle. Make 24 center units.

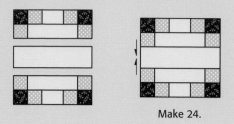

Make 24.

5. Sew two medium tan 2" x 6" rectangles to each side of the center units. Press the seams toward the tan rectangles. Sew two medium tan 2" x 9" rectangles to the top and bottom of the units. Press the seams toward the tan rectangles. You should now have 24 completed center units.

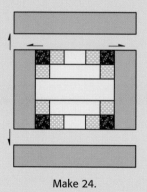

Make 24.

6. Sew one cream triangle to one side of a purple 3½" square, aligning the 90° corners as shown. Press the seams toward the cream triangle. Sew another cream triangle to the adjacent side of the purple square as shown. Press the seams toward the cream triangle. Make 96 triangle units.

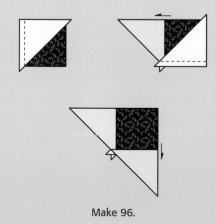

Make 96.

7. Center two triangle units on each side of a center unit from step 5 and sew. Press the seams toward the center unit. Center and sew two triangle units to the remaining sides. Press the seams toward the center unit.

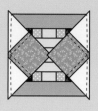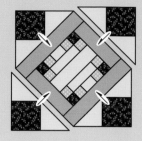

Make 24.

8. I used fusible web and machine appliqué to add the flowers to this quilt, but feel free to use the method of your choice. Refer to "Appliqué" on page 70 for more detailed instructions. Using the patterns on page 22, prepare the flowers and flower centers and appliqué a flower in the center of each block.

9. Trim the block using a 12" square ruler. Measuring 5½" from the center of the block, square the block to 11" x 11". Do your best to line up the purple corner squares at the 2½" mark. Trim all four sides of each block.

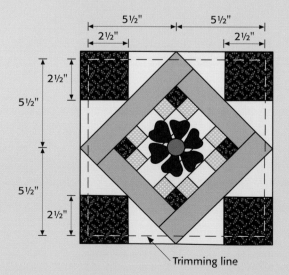

Trimming line

ASSEMBLING THE QUILT

1. Using four red 1½" x 11" sashing strips and five purple 1½" cornerstones for each row, make seven sashing rows as shown. Press the seams toward the sashing strips.

Make 7.

2. Using five red 1½"-wide sashing strips and four blocks for each row, make six block rows. Press the seams toward the sashing strips.

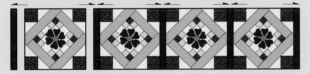

Make 6.

3. Sew the sashing and block rows together. Be sure to match up the 2½" purple squares and block centers, easing when necessary. Press the seams toward the sashing rows.

4. Referring to "Borders" on page 74, attach the 1¾"-wide gold inner border and the 4½"-wide purple outer border to the quilt top.

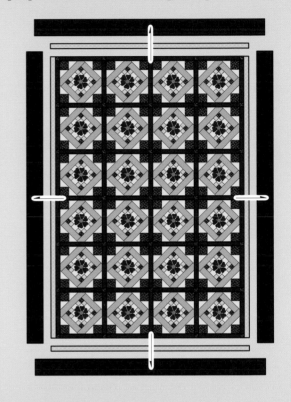

FINISHING THE QUILT

Refer to the quilt finishing techniques on pages 75–79 for more detailed instructions, if needed.

1. Piece the quilt backing so that it's approximately 6" wider and longer than the quilt top. Mark the quilt top if necessary.

2. Layer the quilt top with batting and backing, and baste the layers together. Hand or machine quilt as desired.

3. Trim the batting and backing even with the edges of the quilt top. Add a hanging sleeve if desired. Using the gold 2½"-wide strips, prepare the binding and sew it to the quilt. Make a label and attach it to your quilt.

MARC'S SURPRISE

Designed and pieced by Retta Warehime. Machine quilted by Pam Clarke.
This quilt was made for Marc Connors from Okotoks, Alberta, who lived with our family
for four years during his Western Hockey League career. I made this quilt as a reminder of the years
Marc spent living in the United States and seeing me at the sewing machine, which he called my "desk."

Finished Quilt Size: 57½" x 80½"
Finished Block Size: 10½" x 10½"

MATERIALS

All yardages are based on 42"-wide fabric.

- ★ 1¾ yards of beige print for blocks
- ★ 1½ yards of tan medium-scale print for blocks
- ★ 1⅜ yards of blue print for blocks and cornerstones
- ★ 1⅛ yards of rust print for sashing
- ★ 1⅛ yards of black print for outer border
- ★ ⅞ yard of gold print for blocks and inner border
- ★ ⅜ yard of red print for stars
- ★ ¾ yard of striped fabric for binding*
- ★ 5 yards of fabric for backing
- ★ 64" x 87" piece of batting
- ★ ⅞ yard of lightweight fusible web for appliqué

*You will need 1 yard of striped fabric if you wish to use bias-cut binding rather than straight-cut binding.

CUTTING

From the blue print, cut:
- ★ 4 strips, 1½" x 42"
- ★ 9 strips, 3½" x 42"; crosscut into 96 squares, 3½" x 3½"
- ★ 2 strips, 1½" x 42"; crosscut into 35 squares, 1½" x 1½"

From the gold print, cut:
- ★ 8 strips, 1½" x 42"
- ★ 6 strips, 1¾" x 42"

From the beige print, cut:
- ★ 2 strips, 2" x 42"
- ★ 2 strips, 4" x 42"
- ★ 4 strips, 2" x 42"; crosscut into 24 rectangles, 2" x 6"
- ★ 9 strips, 3⅜" x 42"; crosscut into 96 squares, 3⅜" x 3⅜". Cut once diagonally to yield 192 triangles.

From the tan print, cut:
- ★ 3 strips, 6" x 42"; crosscut into 48 rectangles, 2" x 6"
- ★ 3 strips, 9" x 42"; crosscut into 48 rectangles, 2" x 9"

From the rust print:
- ★ 3 strips, 11" x 42"; crosscut into 58 rectangles, 1½" x 11"

From the black print, cut:
- ★ 7 strips, 4½" x 42"

From the striped fabric, cut**:
- ★ 8 strips, 2½" x 42"

**For straight-cut binding, cut strips across the width of the fabric. If you wish to use bias binding as I did for this quilt, you will cut 2½"-wide strips on the bias and join them end to end to make a continuous strip at least 290" long.

MAKING THE QUILT

Refer to the directions for "Caitlyn's Garden," beginning on page 17, to assemble this quilt. Note that you will appliqué a star (see pattern on page 23) in the center of each block instead of a flower.

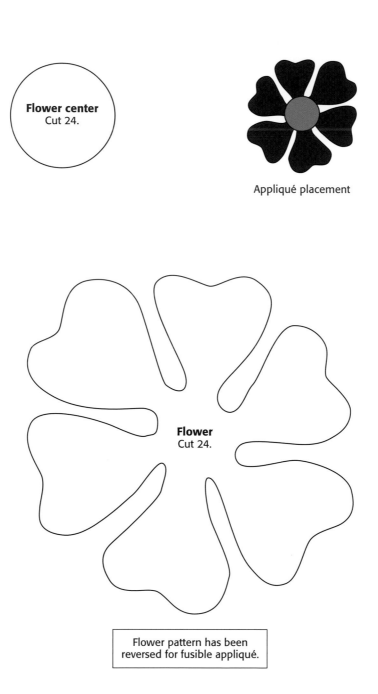

Flower center
Cut 24.

Appliqué placement

Flower
Cut 24.

Flower pattern has been
reversed for fusible appliqué.

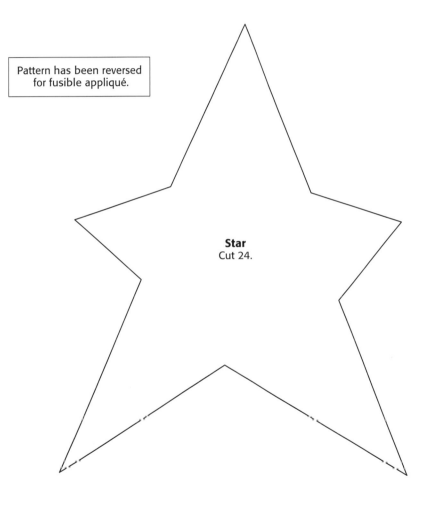

Pattern has been reversed
for fusible appliqué.

Star
Cut 24.

SWEET 'N' TART

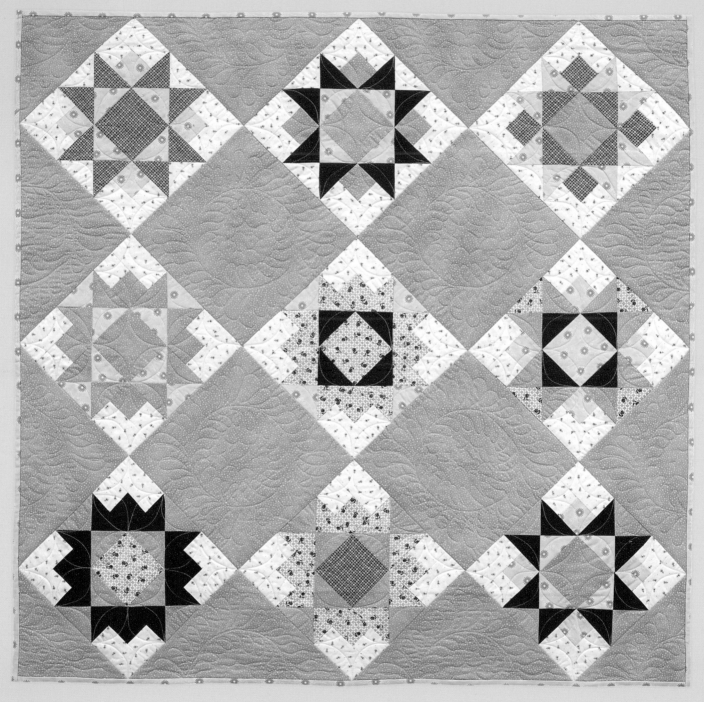

Designed and pieced by Retta Warehime. Quilted by Amy Smith.
Bright jellybean colors make this a happy quilt, appealing to both boys and girls.
I made this version for my great-niece Lauren Paige Lee. Welcome to our family, Lauren!

MATERIALS

All yardages are based on 42"-wide fabric.

* ¼ yard *each* of 7 bright-colored fabrics for blocks (You can introduce scraps, too!)
* 1½ yards of green print for setting blocks, side triangles, and corner triangles
* ¾ yard of cream print for blocks
* ⅝ yard of fabric for binding
* 3¼ yards of fabric for backing
* 57" x 57" piece of batting

CUTTING

From the 7 bright-colored fabrics, you will choose different ones to use as various pieces for each of the blocks.

From the bright-colored fabrics, cut these pieces to make 1 block:

* 1 square, 5¼" x 5¼", for piece A
* 2 squares of the same fabric, 5¼" x 5¼", for piece B
* 1 square, 5¼" x 5¼", for piece C
* 4 squares of the same fabric, 2½" x 2½", for piece D
* 1 square, 4½" x 4½", for center

From the cream print, cut these pieces to make all 9 blocks:

* 3 strips, 4½" x 42"; crosscut into 36 rectangles, 2½" x 4½"
* 3 strips, 2½" x 42"; crosscut into 36 squares, 2½" x 2½"

From the green print, cut:

* 2 squares, 19½" x 19½"; cut twice diagonally to yield 8 side triangles
* 4 squares, 12½" x 12½"
* 2 squares, 10" x 10"; cut once diagonally to yield 4 corner triangles

From the binding fabric, cut:

* 6 strips, 2½" x 42"

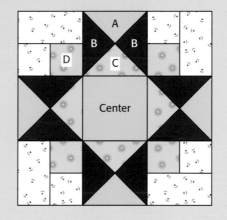

MAKING THE BLOCK

1. Place the 5¼" square for piece A and one 5¼" square for piece B right sides together. With piece B on top, draw a diagonal line twice, corner to corner. Sew ¼" to the left of the drawn lines as shown. Cut on both drawn lines and press the seams toward piece B. Make four of unit 1.

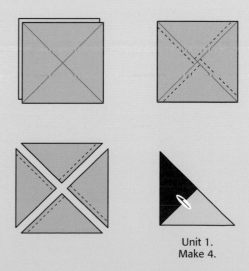

Unit 1.
Make 4.

2. Place the other 5¼" square for piece B and the 5¼" square for piece C right sides together. With piece B on top, draw a diagonal line twice, corner to corner. Sew ¼" to the left of the drawn lines as shown. Cut on both drawn lines and press the seams toward piece B. Make four of unit 2.

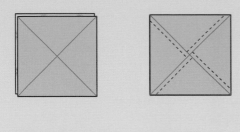

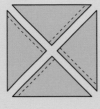

Unit 2.
Make 4.

3. Sew each unit 1 to a unit 2 to make four quarter-square-triangle units.

Make 4.

4. Sew four of the cream 2½" squares to the 2½" squares for piece D. Press the seams toward piece D. Sew a cream 2½" x 4½" rectangle to each of these units as shown. Press the seams toward the rectangle. Make four corner units.

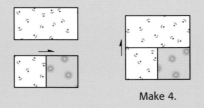

Make 4.

5. Using the quarter-square-triangle units, the corner units, and the 4½" center square, lay out the block as shown. Sew the units into rows, pressing as shown. Sew the rows together and press the seams toward the center row.

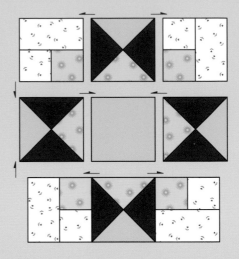

6. For each of the eight remaining blocks, choose another set of bright-colored fabrics from which to cut the pieces, and repeat steps 1–5 to make the blocks.

ASSEMBLING THE QUILT TOP

1. Referring to "Diagonal Settings" on page 73, lay out the pieced blocks, green print 12½" squares, and side triangles.

2. Sew the blocks, squares, and side triangles into rows. Press the seams toward the green print squares.

3. Sew the rows together and press the seams in one direction. Add the 10" corner triangles last, and press the seams toward the corners.

4. Trim the edges ¼" from the block points all around the outside edges of the quilt and square up the corners. Stay stitch around the perimeter of the quilt top ⅛" from the outside edge, taking care not to stretch the edges.

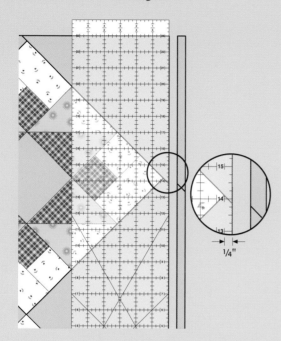

FINISHING THE QUILT

Refer to the quilt finishing techniques on pages 75–79 for more detailed instructions, if needed.

1. Piece the quilt backing so that it's approximately 6" wider and longer than the quilt top. Mark the quilt top if necessary.

2. Layer the quilt top with batting and backing, and baste the layers together. Hand or machine quilt as desired.

3. Trim the batting and backing even with the edges of the quilt top. Add a hanging sleeve if desired. Using the 2½"-wide binding strips, prepare the binding and sew it to the quilt. Make a label and attach it to your quilt.

EXTRA PROJECT

For a great project, make an extra block and sew the block to a beach bag or overnight bag to go along with the quilt. For a bedroom ensemble, turn extra blocks into throw pillows.

RED 'N' HOT

Designed and pieced by Retta Warehime. Quilted by Amy Smith.
This bright-colored quilt reminded me of the bright and optimistic personality of my friend Heather.
This quilt is for her husband, Terry Layden.

MATERIALS

All yardages are based on 42"-wide fabric.

★ ¼ yard *each* of 7 bright-colored fabrics for blocks (You can introduce scraps, too!)
★ 1½ yards of red print for setting blocks, side triangles, and corner triangles
★ ¾ yard of cream print for blocks
★ ⅝ yard of fabric for binding
★ 3¼ yards of fabric for backing
★ 57" x 57" piece of batting

CUTTING

From the 7 bright-colored fabrics, you will choose different ones to use as various pieces for each of the blocks.

From the bright-colored fabrics, cut these pieces to make 1 block:

★ 1 square, 5¼" x 5¼", for piece A
★ 2 squares of the same fabric, 5¼" x 5¼", for piece B
★ 1 square, 5¼" x 5¼", for piece C
★ 4 squares of the same fabric, 2½" x 2½", for piece D
★ 1 square, 4½" x 4½", for center

From the cream print, cut these pieces to make all 9 blocks:

★ 3 strips, 4½" x 42"; crosscut into 36 rectangles, 2½" x 4½"
★ 3 strips, 2½" x 42"; crosscut into 36 squares, 2½" x 2½"

From the red print, cut:

★ 2 squares, 19½" x 19½"; cut twice diagonally to yield 8 side triangles
★ 4 squares, 12½" x 12½"
★ 2 squares, 10" x 10"; cut once diagonally to yield 4 corner triangles

From the binding fabric, cut:

★ 6 strips, 2½" x 42"

MAKING THE QUILT

Refer to the directions for "Sweet 'n' Tart," beginning on page 25, to assemble this quilt.

TWO STARS RISING

Designed and pieced by Retta Warehime. Machine quilted by Pam Clarke.
In red-white-and-blue sets, these sailing ships are off to sea. With "Two Stars Rising,"
your young mariner will be proud and accomplished as the admiral of his own fleet.
I made this quilt for Caleb Michael Elfering.

Finished Quilt Size: 53¼" x 74¾"
Finished Block Size: 10" x 10"

MATERIALS

All yardages are based on 42"-wide fabric.

* 2¼ yards of cream polka-dot fabric for blocks and sashing
* 1¾ yards of rust print for blocks, cornerstones, and outer border
* 1½ yards of black print for blocks and inner border
* ½ yard of tan print for blocks
* ⅜ yard of blue print for boats
* ¼ yard of green print for sails
* ⅛ yard or scrap of gold print for stars
* ⅛ yard or scrap of red print for flags
* ⅝ yard of fabric for binding
* 3½ yards of fabric for backing
* 60" x 81" piece of batting
* 1 yard of lightweight fusible web for appliqué

CUTTING

From the tan print, cut:
* 3 strips, 4½" x 42"; crosscut into 24 squares, 4½" x 4½"

From the cream print, cut:
* 55 strips, 1¼" x 42"; crosscut into:
    * 58 rectangles, 1¼" x 10½"
    * 48 rectangles, 1¼" x 9"
    * 48 rectangles, 1¼" x 7½"
    * 48 rectangles, 1¼" x 6"
    * 48 rectangles, 1¼" x 4½"

From the rust print, cut:
* 20 strips, 1¼" x 42"; crosscut into:
    * 48 rectangles, 1¼" x 7½"
    * 48 rectangles, 1¼" x 6"
    * 35 squares, 1¼" x 1¼"
* 7 strips, 4" x 42"

From the black print, cut:
* 28 strips, 1¼" x 42"; crosscut into:
    * 48 rectangles, 1¼" x 10½"
    * 48 rectangles, 1¼" x 9"
* 6 strips, 1¾" x 42"

From the binding fabric, cut;
* 7 strips, 2½" x 42"

MAKING THE BLOCKS

1. Beginning with a tan print 4½" square and using the illustration as a guide for strip length and color, assemble the pieces in numerical order. Press the seams away from the center after adding each strip.

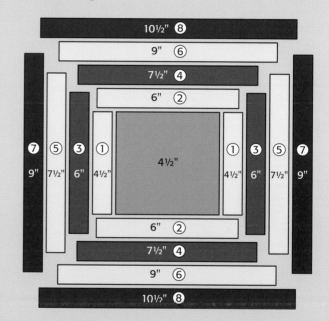

Make 24.

2. I used fusible web and machine appliqué to add the sailboats and stars to this quilt, but feel free to use the method of your choice. Refer to "Appliqué" on page 70 for more detailed instructions. Using the patterns on page 33, prepare the boats, sails, small stars, flags, and large stars for appliqué. Machine appliqué a sailboat to 22 of the blocks and a large star to the remaining 2 blocks as shown.

Make 22.   Make 2.

ASSEMBLING THE QUILT TOP

1. Using 28 of the cream 10½"-long rectangles and all of the rust 1¼"-square cornerstones, assemble seven sashing rows. Press the seams toward the sashing strips.

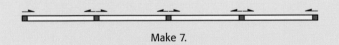

Make 7.

2. Using four blocks and five cream 10½" rectangles for each row, assemble six block rows. Press the seams toward the sashing strips. The two blocks with stars should be placed in the bottom row on the right.

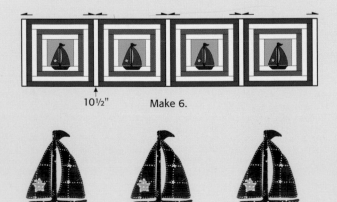

10½"   Make 6.

3. Sew the block rows and the sashing rows together. Press the seams toward the sashing rows. Be sure the appliqué motifs are upright as you sew the rows together.

4. Referring to "Borders" on page 74, attach the 1¾"-wide black inner border and the 4"-wide rust outer border to the quilt top.

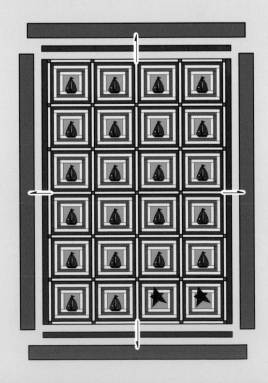

FINISHING THE QUILT

Refer to the quilt finishing techniques on pages 75–79 for more detailed instructions, if needed.

1. Piece the quilt backing so that it's approximately 6" wider and longer than the quilt top. Mark the quilt top if necessary.

2. Layer the quilt top with batting and backing, and baste the layers together. Hand or machine quilt as desired.

3. Trim the batting and backing even with the edges of the quilt top. Add a hanging sleeve if desired. Using the 2½"-wide binding strips, prepare the binding and sew it to the quilt. Make a label and attach it to your quilt.

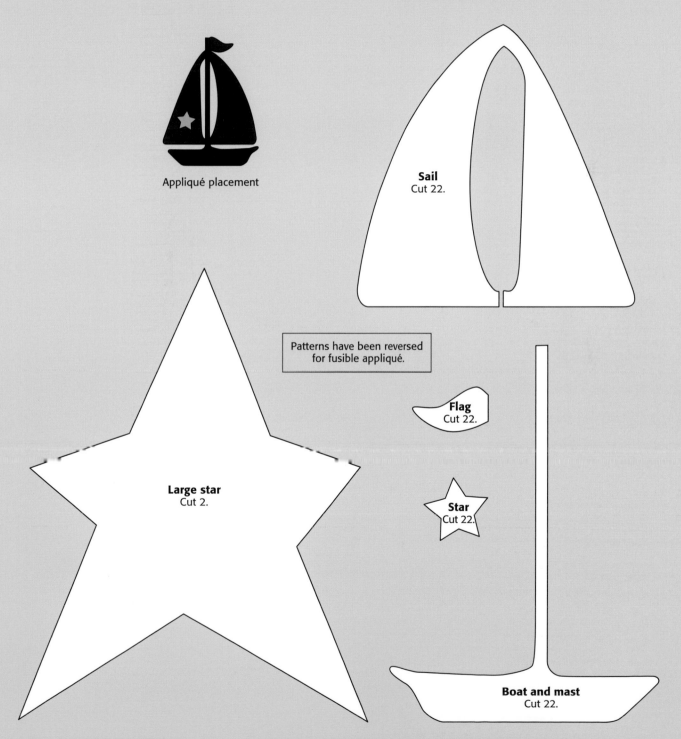

Appliqué placement

Sail
Cut 22.

Patterns have been reversed for fusible appliqué.

Large star
Cut 2.

Flag
Cut 22.

Star
Cut 22.

Boat and mast
Cut 22.

WHITNEY'S WHIMSY

Designed and pieced by Retta Warehime. Machine quilted by Pam Clarke.

This quilt will be given to my granddaughter Whitney Diana Holland. When she was little she would always ask to have her "drends" come over and play. Of course "drends" meant "friends." Knowing that ladybugs are a symbol of friendship, it was fun to create this whimsical quilt for Whitney and her "drends."

Finished Quilt Size: 58¼" x 79¾"
Finished Block Size: 10" x 10"

MATERIALS

All yardages are based on 42"-wide fabric.

- ★ 2½ yards of gold print for blocks, inner border, and outer border
- ★ 2¼ yards of yellow print for blocks and sashing
- ★ 1⅛ yards of green print for flower centers, middle border, and binding
- ★ ⅞ yard of melon print for blocks and cornerstones
- ★ ½ yard of gold checked fabric for blocks
- ★ ½ yard of dark melon print for flowers and ladybugs
- ★ ⅛ yard or scrap of black fabric for ladybug heads
- ★ 5 yards of fabric for backing
- ★ 65" x 86" piece of batting
- ★ 1 yard of lightweight fusible web for appliqué
- ★ Black embroidery floss

CUTTING

From the gold checked fabric, cut:
- ★ 3 strips, 4½" x 42"; crosscut into 24 squares, 4½" x 4½"

From the yellow print, cut:
- ★ 55 strips, 1¼" x 42"; crosscut into:
  - · 58 rectangles 1¼" x 10½"
  - · 48 rectangles, 1¼" x 9"
  - · 48 rectangles, 1¼" x 7½"
  - · 48 rectangles, 1¼" x 6"
  - · 48 rectangles, 1¼" x 4½"

From the melon print, cut:
- ★ 20 strips, 1¼" x 42"; crosscut into:
  - · 48 rectangles, 1¼" x 7½"
  - · 48 rectangles, 1¼" x 6"
  - · 35 squares, 1¼" x 1¼"

From the gold print, cut:
- ★ 28 strips, 1¼" x 42"; crosscut into:
  - · 48 rectangles, 1¼" x 10½"
  - · 48 rectangles, 1¼" x 9"
- ★ 6 strips, 1¾" x 42"
- ★ 7 strips, 4½" x 42"

From the green print, cut;
- ★ 6 strips, 2½" x 42"
- ★ 8 binding strips, 2½" x 42"

MAKING THE QUILT

1. Referring to step 1 of "Making the Blocks" on page 31, piece 24 blocks.

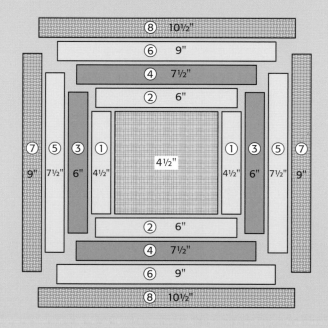

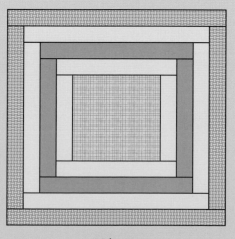

Make 24.

2. I used fusible web and machine appliqué to add the flowers and ladybugs to this quilt, but feel free to use the method of your choice. Refer to "Appliqué" on page 70 for more detailed instructions. Using the patterns on page 37, prepare the flowers and flower centers, and the ladybug bodies, heads, and antenna tips for appliqué. Machine appliqué a flower to 12 of the blocks and a ladybug to the remaining 12 blocks as shown. Using three strands of black embroidery floss, stitch several French knots in the flower centers, and backstitch two antennae and a wing line on each of the ladybugs.

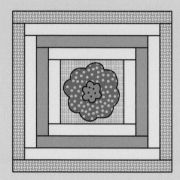

Make 12.

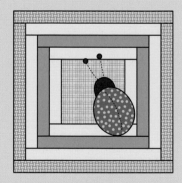

Make 12.

3. Referring to steps 1–3 of "Assembling the Quilt Top" on page 32, piece the quilt center.

4. Referring to "Borders" on page 74, attach the 1¾"-wide gold print inner border, the 2½"-wide green print middle border, and the 4½"-wide gold print outer border to the quilt top.

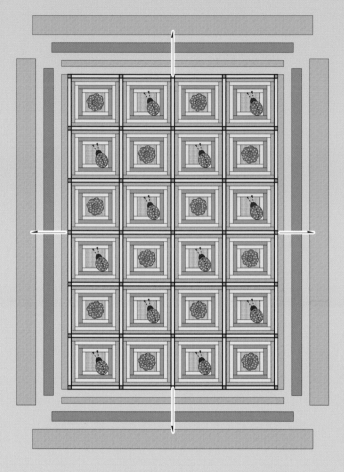

5. Referring to "Finishing the Quilt" on page 33, complete your quilt.

French knot

Backstitch

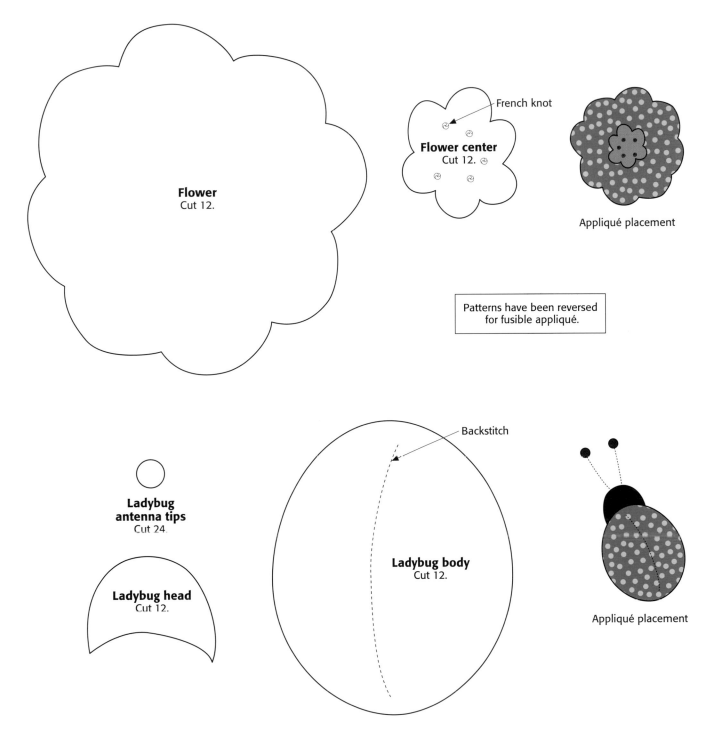

Flower
Cut 12.

French knot

Flower center
Cut 12.

Appliqué placement

Patterns have been reversed
for fusible appliqué.

Backstitch

**Ladybug
antenna tips**
Cut 24.

Ladybug head
Cut 12.

Ladybug body
Cut 12.

Appliqué placement

KICKIN' KITES

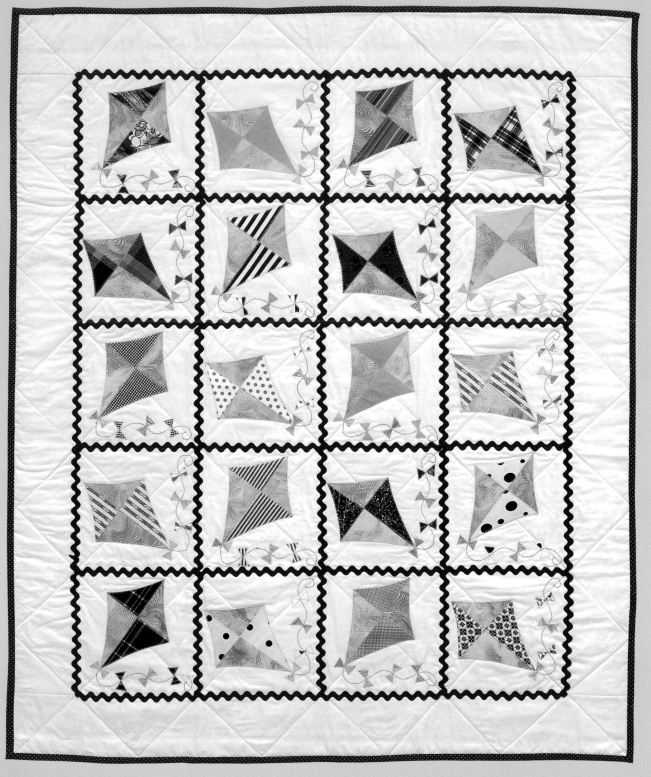

By Retta Warehime

Gusty spring winds kick up some fun with these colorful kites. I used my grandmother's old fabrics for the kites and combined them with the same kite background fabric to make this quilt up quick. I love the big rickrack!

Finished Quilt Size: 40" x 48"
Finished Block Size: 8" x 8"

MATERIALS

All yardages are based on 42"-wide fabric.

★ 2⅛ yards of muslin for blocks and border
★ ⅞ yard of gold fabric for kites and tail ties
★ 5" x 5" square *each* of 20 different fabrics for kites and tail ties
★ ½ yard of red print for binding
★ 3 yards of fabric for backing
★ 46" x 54" piece of batting
★ 3 yards of lightweight fusible web for appliqué
★ 12 yards of red rickrack
★ Blue embroidery floss

CUTTING

From the muslin, cut:
★ 20 squares, 8½" x 8½"
★ 5 strips, 4½" x 42"

From the red print, cut:
★ 5 strips, 2½" x 42"

MAKING THE BLOCKS

I used fusible web and machine appliqué to add the kites and tail ties to this quilt, but feel free to use the method of your choice. Refer to "Appliqué" on page 70 for more detailed instructions. Using the patterns on page 41, prepare the kite pieces and the tail ties for appliqué. Machine appliqué a kite and four tail ties on the center of each 8½" muslin square. Using three strands of blue embroidery floss, backstitch a tail for each kite (see backstitch diagram on page 36).

ASSEMBLING THE QUILT TOP

1. Lay out the blocks in five rows of four blocks each. Change the direction the kites are flying by rotating the blocks.

2. Sew the blocks together into rows, and press the seams in opposite directions from row to row. Sew the rows together and press the seams in one direction.

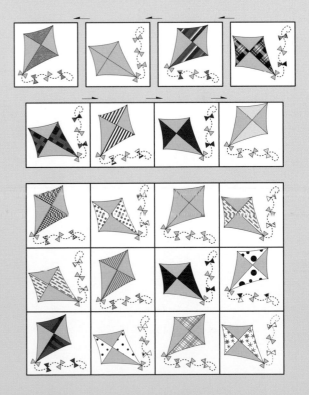

3. Referring to "Borders" on page 74, attach the 4½"-wide muslin border to the quilt top.

FINISHING THE QUILT

Refer to the quilt finishing techniques on pages 75–79 for more detailed instructions, if needed.

1. Piece the quilt backing so that it's approximately 6" wider and longer than the quilt top. Mark the quilt top if necessary.

2. Layer the quilt top with batting and backing, and baste the layers together. Stitch the rickrack to all the inside horizontal and vertical block seam lines. Then stitch the rickrack all around the border seam lines as shown, covering the ends of the rickrack in the rows.

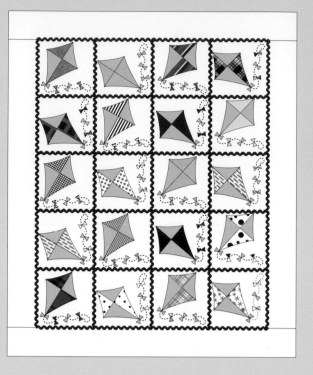

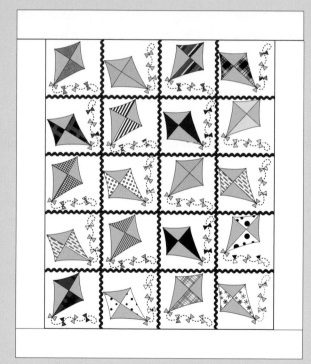

3. Trim the batting and backing even with the edges of the quilt top. Add a hanging sleeve if desired. Using the red print 2½"-wide strips, prepare the binding and sew it to the quilt. Make a label and attach it to your quilt.

PILLOWS

Cut two extra muslin 8½" squares and add an appliqué motif to the center of one square. Place the muslin squares right sides together, position large rickrack between the layers along the edges to make a cute pillow trim, and pin. Leave an opening for turning and sew a ¼" seam around the perimeter of the pillow. Trim the corners, turn the pillow right side out, and stuff lightly. Slipstitch the opening closed. Throw three or four pillows in a crib, on the bed, or in a basket.

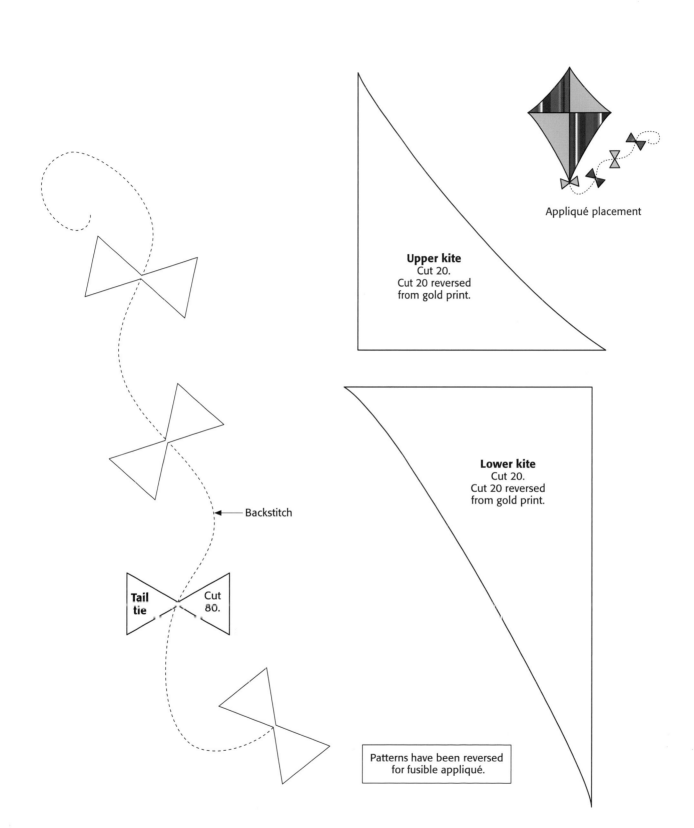

Appliqué placement

Upper kite
Cut 20.
Cut 20 reversed
from gold print.

Lower kite
Cut 20.
Cut 20 reversed
from gold print.

Backstitch

Tail tie
Cut 80.

Patterns have been reversed
for fusible appliqué.

PERFECT POSIES

By Retta Warehime

Inspired by sentimental memories of my grandma's springtime flowers, perfect posies are potted
in happy pairs and will lift your spirits. Special nostalgic fabrics, all scraps from my grandma's collection,
were appliquéd into this charming quilt that will be kept in our family.

Finished Quilt Size: 40" x 48"
Finished Block Size: 8" x 8"

MATERIALS

All yardages are based on 42"-wide fabric.

- 2⅛ yards of muslin for blocks and border
- 5" x 5" square *each* of 20 different blue fabrics for pots
- 4" x 4" square *each* of 40 different fabrics for flowers and flower centers
- ½ yard of green print for binding
- 3 yards of fabric for backing
- 46" x 54" piece of batting
- 2½ yards of lightweight fusible web for appliqué
- 12 yards of green rickrack
- Green embroidery floss

CUTTING

From the muslin, cut:
- 20 squares, 8½" x 8½"
- 5 strips, 4½" x 42"

From the green print, cut:
- 5 strips, 2½" x 42"

MAKING THE BLOCKS

I used fusible web and machine appliqué to add the pots of posies to this quilt, but feel free to use the method of your choice. Refer to "Appliqué" on page 70 for more detailed instructions. Using the patterns on page 44, prepare the pots, flowers, and flower centers for appliqué. Machine appliqué a pot and two flowers to the center of each 8½" muslin square. Using three strands of green embroidery floss, backstitch a stem for each flower (see backstitch diagram on page 36).

ASSEMBLING THE QUILT TOP

Referring to "Assembling the Quilt Top" on page 39, piece the quilt center and add the border.

FINISHING THE QUILT

Referring to "Finishing the Quilt" on page 40, complete your quilt, but use the following instructions for adding the rickrack. Stitch the rickrack to all of the vertical block and border seam lines. Then stitch the rickrack to all of the horizontal block and border seam lines as shown, covering the ends of the rickrack in the vertical rows.

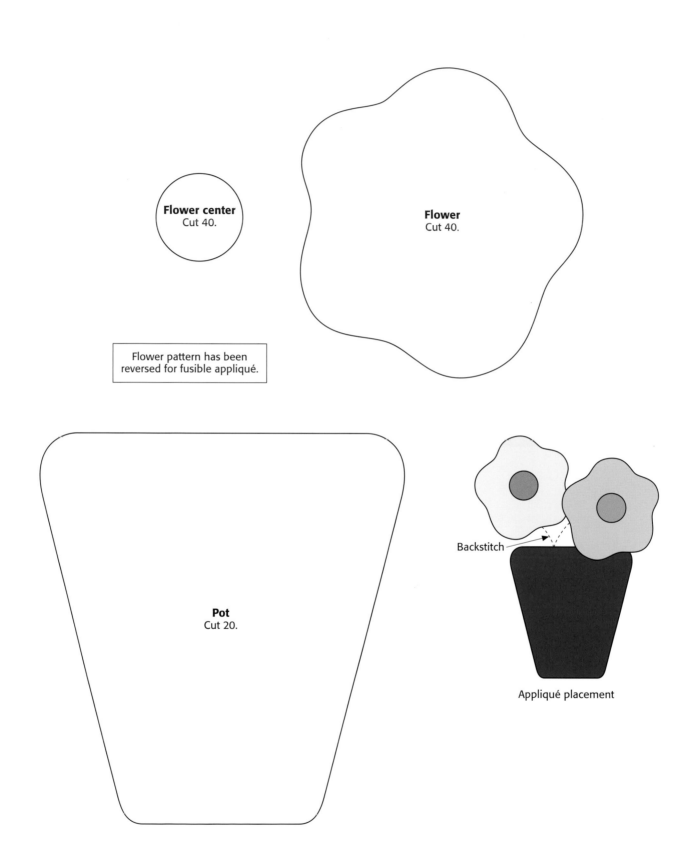

Flower center
Cut 40.

Flower
Cut 40.

Flower pattern has been
reversed for fusible appliqué.

Pot
Cut 20.

Backstitch

Appliqué placement

CANDY FLOSS

By Retta Warehime

Finely spun cotton candy, or candy floss as our Canadian cousins call it, was the inspiration
for this sweet pink girl's quilt. This quilt was donated to the Breast Cancer Research Foundation.

Finished Quilt Size: 57" x 78"
Finished Block Size: 18" x 18"

MATERIALS

All yardages are based on 42"-wide fabric.

- ★ ¾ yard *each* of 7 light to medium prints for blocks and binding
- ★ 2¼ yards of dark pink print for sashing and outer border
- ★ ⅜ yard of medium dark print for inner border
- ★ ¼ yard of medium light print for cornerstones
- ★ 4½ yards of fabric for backing
- ★ 63" x 84" piece of batting

CUTTING

From *each* of the 7 light to medium prints, cut:

- ★ 6 strips, 2½" x 42" (42 total; you will use 36.)
- ★ 2½"-wide binding strips in lengths varying from 12" to 20" (282" total)

From the dark pink print, cut:

- ★ 9 strips, 3½" x 42"; crosscut into 17 rectangles, 3½" x 18½"
- ★ 7 strips, 5½" x 42"

From the medium light print, cut;

- ★ 12 squares, 3½" x 3½"

From the medium dark print cut;

- ★ 6 strips, 1½" x 42"

MAKING THE BLOCKS

1. Using the 2½" x 42" strips of print fabric for blocks, randomly sew nine strips together lengthwise. Reverse your sewing direction as you add each strip. This will keep your strip set from curving. Press the seams in one direction. Make four strip sets. Cut 54 segments, 2½" wide.

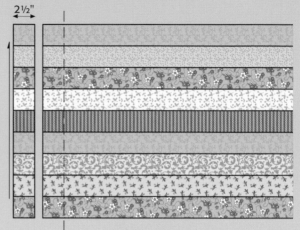

2½"

Make 4 strip sets.
Cut 54 segments.

2. Sew nine segments from step 1 together, reversing your sewing direction as you add each segment. Press the seams to one side. Make six blocks.

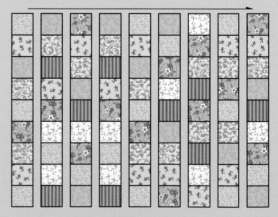

Make 6.

ASSEMBLING THE QUILT TOP

1. Using two dark pink 3½"-wide rectangles and three medium light 3½" cornerstones for each row, make four sashing rows as shown. Press the seams toward the sashing strips.

Make 4.

2. Using three dark pink 3½"-wide rectangles and two blocks for each row, make three block rows. Press the seams toward the sashing strips.

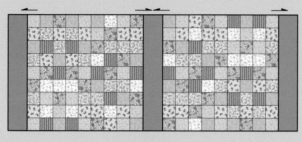

Make 3.

3. Sew the block rows and the sashing rows together. Press the seams toward the sashing rows.

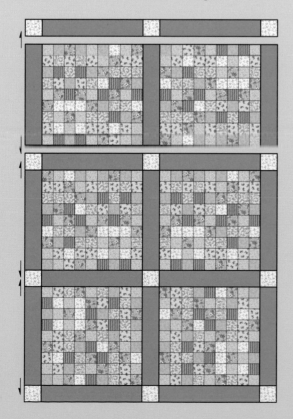

4. Referring to "Borders" on page 74, attach the 1½"-wide medium dark inner border and the 5½"-wide dark pink outer border to the quilt top.

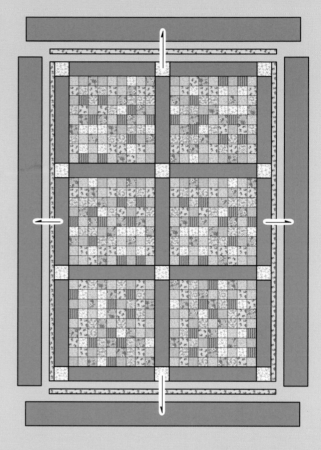

FINISHING THE QUILT

Refer to the quilt finishing techniques on pages 75–79 for more detailed instructions, if needed.

1. Piece the quilt backing so that it's approximately 6" wider and longer than the quilt top. Mark the quilt top if necessary.

2. Layer the quilt top with batting and backing, and baste the layers together. Hand or machine quilt as desired.

3. Trim the batting and backing even with the edges of the quilt top. Add a hanging sleeve if desired. Using the assorted 2½"-wide binding strips, prepare the binding and sew it to the quilt. Make a label and attach it to your quilt.

ROOT BEER FLOAT

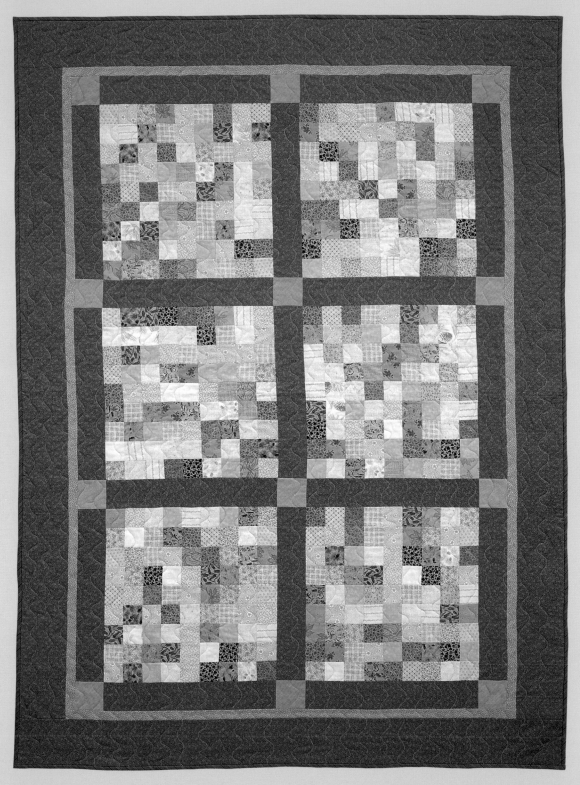

By Retta Warehime

"Root Beer Float" is done in warm browns and soft vanilla colors—yummy and so simple to make!
This quilt was a wedding gift for Heather and Jared Gilbert.

MATERIALS

All yardages are based on 42"-wide fabric.

- ⅝ yard *each* of 7 light to medium dark prints for blocks
- 2¼ yards of dark brown print for sashing and outer border
- ⅜ yard of medium print for inner border
- ¼ yard of medium light print for cornerstones
- ⅝ yard of fabric for binding
- 4½ yards of fabric for backing
- 63" x 84" piece of batting

CUTTING

From *each* of the 7 light to medium dark prints, cut:
- 6 strips, 2½" x 42" (42 total; you will use 36.)

From the dark brown print, cut:
- 9 strips, 3½" x 42"; crosscut into 17 rectangles, 3½" x 18½"
- 7 strips, 5½" x 42"

From the medium light print, cut;
- 12 squares, 3½" x 3½"

From the medium print cut;
- 6 strips, 1½" x 42"

From the binding fabric, cut:
- 7 strips, 2½" x 42"

MAKING THE QUILT

Refer to the directions for "Candy Floss" beginning on page 46 to assemble this quilt.

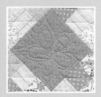

MELODY GREEN

Designed and pieced by Retta Warehime. Quilted by Amy Smith.
Made with three simple blocks, this quilt is much easier to construct than it looks. The soft butter yellows complement the greens in this quick-to-piece quilt. This quilt was made for my niece Trishia and her husband, Myke Isayev, as their wedding gift.

MATERIALS

All yardages are based on 42"-wide fabric.

* 1 yard *each* of 2 dark, 2 medium, and 2 light prints for blocks
* 1¾ yards of medium dark green print for blocks and outer border
* ½ yard of medium gold print for inner border
* ¾ yard of fabric for binding
* 5 yards of fabric for backing
* 74" x 87" piece of batting

CUTTING

From *each* of the dark, medium, and light prints, cut:

* 10 strips, 2½" x 42" (60 total; you will use 55.)
* 3 squares, 2½" x 2½" (18 total; you will use 14.)
* 6 squares, 2⅞" x 2⅞"; cut once diagonally to yield 72 triangles (You will use 70.)

From the medium dark green print, cut:

* 3 strips, 6½" x 42"; crosscut into 18 squares, 6½" x 6½"
* 8 strips, 4½" x 42"

From the medium gold print, cut:

* 7 strips, 1¾" x 42"

From the binding fabric, cut:

* 8 strips, 2½" x 42"

MAKING THE BLOCKS

1. Randomly sew three of the light, medium, or dark 2½"-wide strips together. Press the seams in one direction. Make four of strip set A. From the strip sets, cut 2½"-wide segments to make 50 of segment A.

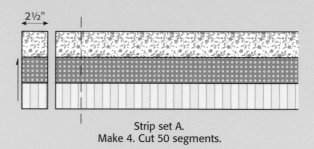

Strip set A.
Make 4. Cut 50 segments.

2. Randomly sew five of the light, medium, or dark 2½"-wide strips together. Press the seams in one direction. Make seven of strip set B. From the strip sets, cut 2½"-wide segments to make 106 of segment B.

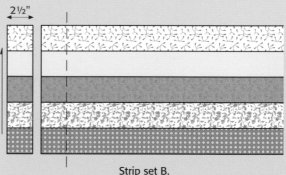

Strip set B.
Make 7. Cut 106 segments.

3. Randomly sew four of the light, medium, or dark 2½"-wide strips together. Press the seams in one direction. Make two of strip set C. From the strip sets, cut 2½"-wide segments to make 21 of segment C.

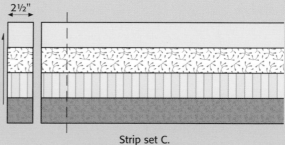

Strip set C.
Make 2. Cut 21 segments.

4. Using 7 of segment C, remove the middle seam as shown to make 14 new segments called segment D, which consist of two squares each.

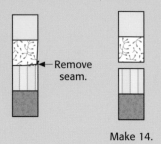

Make 14.

5. To make block 1: Sew one of segment A to each side of a medium dark green 6½" square. Be sure the seams on the segment As are going down. Press the seams you just sewed to the right as shown. Sew a segment B to the top and bottom. The seams on the segment Bs should be going to the left. Press the seams you just sewed toward the bottom of the block. Make 18 of block 1.

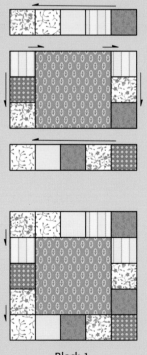

Block 1.
Make 18.

6. To make block 2: Sew five of segment B together, orienting the existing seams of each segment in the direction shown. Press the block seams to the right. Make 14 of block 2.

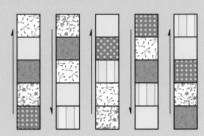

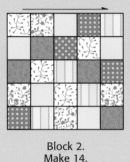

Block 2.
Make 14.

7. To make block 3: Sew the light, medium, and dark 2⅞" triangles to the ends of 14 of segments A, C, and D, and to the light, medium, and dark 2½" squares as shown. Join the rows and add a 2⅞" triangle to the bottom as shown to make 14 of block 3.

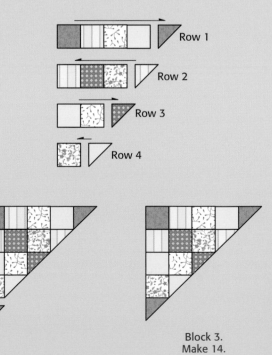

Block 3.
Make 14.

ASSEMBLING THE QUILT TOP

1. Lay out the blocks into diagonal rows, beginning with row 1 in the upper-left corner and ending with row 8 on the bottom right. Sew the blocks into rows and press the seams in opposite directions from row to row. Sew the rows together and press the seams in one direction.

2. Stay stitch around the perimeter of the quilt top ⅛" from the outside edge, taking care not to stretch the edges.

ADDING THE BORDERS

1. Sew the 1¾"-wide medium gold strips end to end. From this long piece, cut four strips, 15" long; two strips, 48" long; and two strips, 62" long.

2. Center and sew the 15"-long strips onto each corner of the quilt top. Press the seams toward the border strips and trim the ends of each strip even with the quilt top.

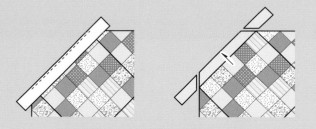

3. Center and sew the 48"-long strips to the top and bottom. Press and trim as above.

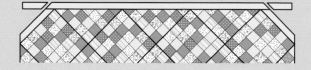

4. Center and sew the 62"-long strips to each side and press and trim as above.

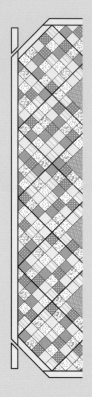

5. Sew the 4½"-wide medium dark green strips end to end. From this long piece, cut four strips, 20" long; two strips, 54" long; and two strips, 68" long. Repeat steps 2–3 to attach these outer-border strips to the quilt top.

FINISHING THE QUILT

Refer to the quilt finishing techniques on pages 75–79 for more detailed instructions, if needed.

1. Piece the quilt backing so that it's approximately 6" wider and longer than the quilt top. Mark the quilt top if necessary.

2. Layer the quilt top with batting and backing, and baste the layers together. Hand or machine quilt as desired.

3. Trim the batting and backing even with the edges of the quilt top. Add a hanging sleeve if desired. Using the 2½"-wide binding strips, prepare the binding and sew it to the quilt. Make a label and attach it to your quilt.

EASTERN SWING BLUE

Designed and pieced by Retta Warehime. Machine quilted by Amy Smith.
Use scraps from your scrap basket or purchase new fabrics—either way your quilt will be a hit!
This quilt was made for my grandson Cole Phillip Holland, who is an awesome little hockey player.

Finished Quilt Size: 67" x 81¼"
Finished Block Size: 10" x 10"

MATERIALS

All yardages are based on 42"-wide fabric.

★ 1 yard *each* of 2 dark, 2 medium, and 2 light prints for blocks

★ 1¾ yards of medium dark blue print for blocks and outer border

★ ½ yard of medium beige print for inner border

★ ¾ yard of fabric for binding

★ 5 yards of fabric for backing

★ 74" x 87" piece of batting

CUTTING

From *each* of the dark, medium, and light prints, cut:

★ 10 strips, 2½" x 42" (60 total; you will use 55.)

★ 3 squares, 2½" x 2½" (18 total; you will use 14.)

★ 6 squares, 2⅞" x 2⅞"; cut once diagonally to yield 72 triangles (You will use 70.)

From the medium dark blue print, cut:

★ 3 strips, 6½" x 42"; crosscut into 18 squares, 6½" x 6½"

★ 8 strips, 4½" x 42"

From the medium beige print, cut:

★ 7 strips, 1¾" x 42"

From the binding fabric, cut:

★ 8 strips, 2½" x 42"

MAKING THE QUILT

Refer to the directions for "Melody Green" beginning on page 51 to assemble this quilt.

SKY HIGH

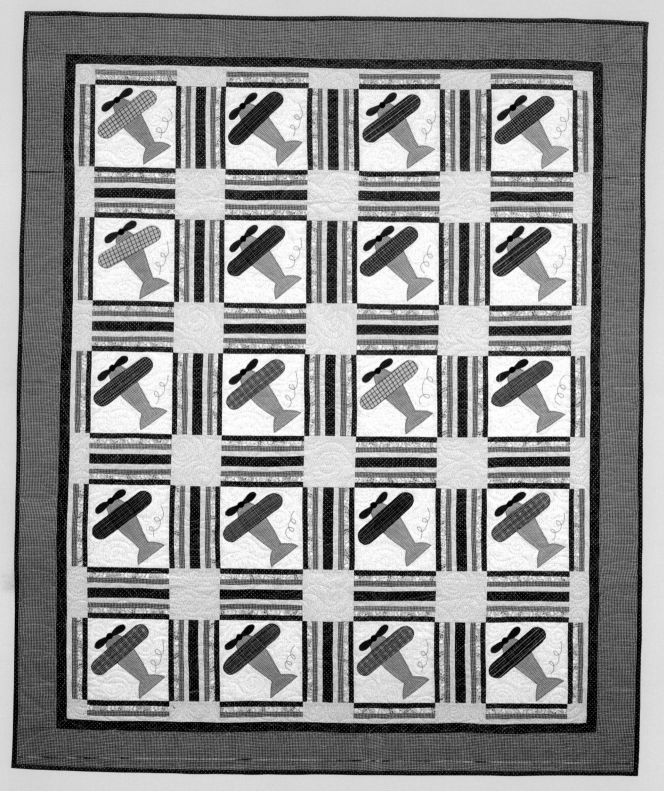

Designed and pieced by Retta Warehime. Machine quilted by Pam Clarke.

Boys fly high in these sky-blue planes. Is he a crop duster or a stunt pilot at an air show? This quilt makes a special place for his imagination to grow. This quilt goes to my newest grandson, Kage Daniel Ballard; it is his first quilt.

MATERIALS

All yardages are based on 42"-wide fabric.

* ¾ yard *each* of 2 light fabrics and 1 medium fabric for sashing
* 1½ yards of cream print for blocks
* 1½ yards of dark blue pin-dot fabric for sashing and inner border
* 1 fat quarter *each* of 5 different blue prints for wings
* 1 yard of medium blue checked or plaid fabric for outer border
* ¾ yard of medium cream print for cornerstones
* ½ yard of light blue fabric for airplane bodies
* 1 fat quarter of red fabric for props
* ⅛ yard or scrap of black fabric for prop centers
* ⅝ yard of fabric for binding
* 4 yards of fabric for backing
* 67" x 80" piece of batting
* 1⅝ yards of lightweight fusible web for appliqué
* Blue embroidery floss

CUTTING

From the cream print, cut:
* 20 squares, 8½" x 8½"

From the dark blue pin-dot fabric, cut:
* 20 strips, 1" x 42"
* 2 strips, 8½" x 42"; crosscut into 31 pieces, 1½" x 8½"
* 6 strips, 1½" x 42"

From *each* of the 2 light fabrics and 1 medium fabric, cut:
* 20 strips, 1" x 42"

From the medium cream print, cut:
* 4 strips, 5½" x 42"; crosscut into:
  * 12 squares, 5½" x 5½"
  * 14 pieces, 2½" x 5½"
* 4 squares, 2½" x 2½"

From the blue checked or plaid fabric, cut:
* 7 strips, 4½" x 42"

From the binding fabric, cut:
* 7 strips, 2½" x 42"

MAKING THE BLOCKS

I used fusible web and machine appliqué to add the airplanes to this quilt, but feel free to use the method of your choice. Refer to "Appliqué" on page 70 for more detailed instructions. Using the patterns on pages 62–63, prepare the airplane bodies, wings, props, and prop centers for appliqué. Machine appliqué an airplane to the center of each cream print 8½" square. Using three strands of blue embroidery floss, backstitch a vapor trail behind each airplane (see backstitch diagram on page 36).

ASSEMBLING THE QUILT TOP

1. Sew a dark, first light, medium, and second light 1" x 42" strip together lengthwise. Press the seams toward the dark strip. Make 20 identical strip sets. Cut the strip sets into 80 segments, 8½" wide.

Make 20 strip sets.
Cut 80 segments.

2. Make 16 sashing units using 32 of the 8½"-wide pieced segments from step 1 and 16 of the dark blue 1½" x 8½" strips. Be sure to place the dark blue strip in the pieced segment to the outside as shown. Sew a pieced segment to each side of a dark blue strip. Press the seams toward the pieced segments.

Make 16.

3. Make four interior sashing rows using eight of the medium cream 2½" x 5½" pieces, the medium cream 5½" squares, and the units from step 2. Sew the pieces together and press the seams as shown.

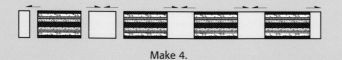

Make 4.

4. Make one each of the top and bottom sashing rows using eight of the 8½"-wide pieced segments from step 1, the remaining medium cream 2½" x 5½" pieces, and the four medium cream 2½" squares. Be sure to place the dark blue strip in the pieced segment in the same position across the row. Sew the pieces together and press the seams as shown.

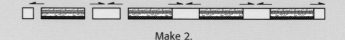

Make 2.

5. Sew an 8½"-wide pieced segment from step 1 to the sides of each appliqué block as shown and press the seams toward the block. Be sure to place the dark blue strip in the pieced segment next to the block.

Make 20.

6. Make five block rows using the units from step 5 and the dark blue 1½" x 8½" strips. Be sure all the airplanes are flying in the same direction. Sew the pieces together and press the seams as shown.

Make 5.

7. Join the block rows, interior sashing rows, and top and bottom sashing rows as shown to complete the quilt top. Be sure the dark strips are next to the blocks when adding the top and bottom sashing rows. Press all the seams toward the sashing rows.

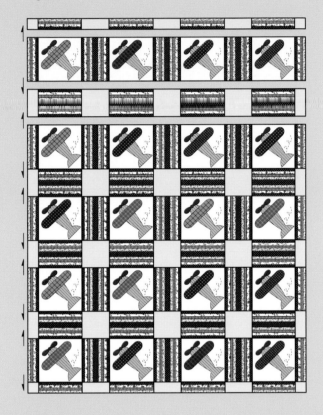

8. Referring to "Borders" on page 74, attach the 1½"-wide dark blue inner border and the 4½"-wide medium blue checked or plaid outer border to the quilt top.

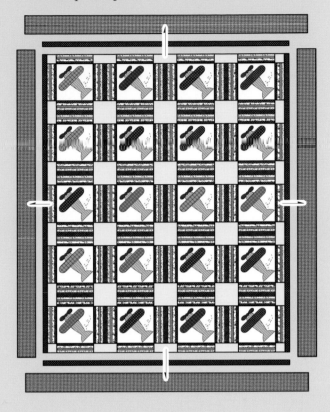

FINISHING THE QUILT

Refer to the quilt finishing techniques on pages 75–79 for more detailed instructions, if needed.

1. Piece the quilt backing so that it's approximately 6" wider and longer than the quilt top. Mark the quilt top if necessary.

2. Layer the quilt top with batting and backing, and baste the layers together. Hand or machine quilt as desired.

3. Trim the batting and backing even with the edges of the quilt top. Add a hanging sleeve if desired. Using the 2½"-wide binding strips, prepare the binding and sew it to the quilt. Make a label and attach it to your quilt.

PAINTED ADDITIONS

Nothing could be cuter than matching up the quilt fabric colors with acrylic paints, and then using the placement guide as a pattern, transferring the motifs onto a wall, bedpost, window shade, or toy box to accessorize a child's room.

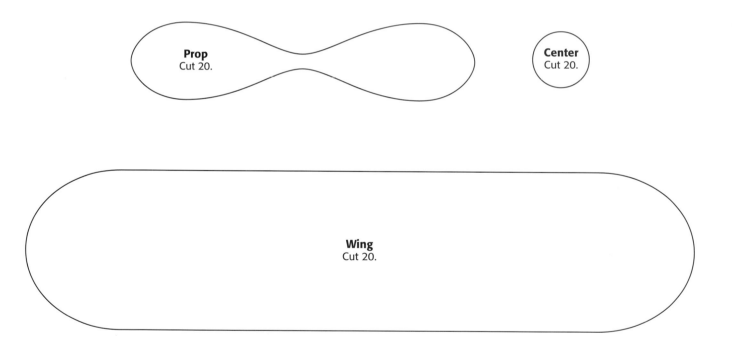

Prop
Cut 20.

Center
Cut 20.

Wing
Cut 20.

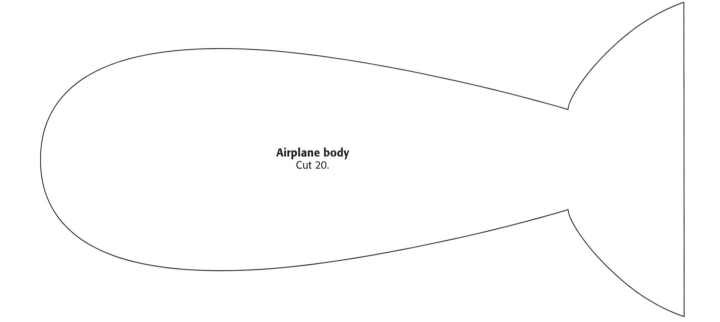

Airplane body
Cut 20.

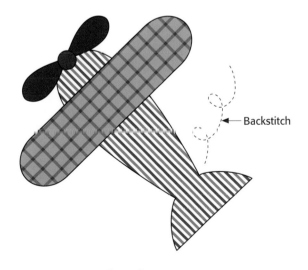

Backstitch

Appliqué placement

MAKAYLA BUGS

Designed and pieced by Retta Warehime. Machine quilted by Pam Clarke.

"Makayla Bugs" gives smiles and hugs to anyone who cuddles up to this delightful girl's quilt.

Bright, buzzy fabrics bounce from square to square in this scrappy delight. This quilt was made for my granddaughter Makayla Lynne Gilbert, my little "Makayla bug."

MATERIALS

All yardages are based on 42"-wide fabric.

- ★ 1 fat quarter *each* of 10 different fabrics for butterfly wings
- ★ ¾ yard *each* of 2 light fabrics and 1 medium fabric for sashing
- ★ 1½ yards of cream small-scale print for blocks
- ★ 1½ yards of dark red print for sashing and inner border
- ★ 1 yard of floral print for outer border
- ★ ¾ yard of cream medium-scale print for cornerstones
- ★ ⅛ yard or scrap of blue fabric for butterfly bodies
- ★ ⅝ yard of fabric for binding
- ★ 4 yards of fabric for backing
- ★ 67" x 80" piece of batting
- ★ 1½ yards of lightweight fusible web for appliqué
- ★ Blue embroidery floss

CUTTING

From the cream small-scale print, cut:
- ★ 20 squares, 8½" x 8½"

From the dark red print, cut:
- ★ 20 strips, 1" x 42"
- ★ 2 strips, 8½" x 42"; crosscut into 31 pieces, 1½" x 8½"
- ★ 6 strips, 1½" x 42"

From *each* of the 2 light fabrics and 1 medium fabric, cut:
- ★ 20 strips, 1" x 42"

From the cream medium-scale print, cut:
- ★ 4 strips, 5½" x 42"; crosscut into:
  - · 12 squares, 5½" x 5½"
  - · 14 pieces, 2½" x 5½"
- ★ 4 squares, 2½" x 2½"

From the floral print, cut:
- ★ 7 strips, 4½" x 42"

From the binding fabric, cut:
- ★ 7 strips, 2½" x 42"

MAKING THE QUILT

Refer to the directions for "Sky High," beginning on page 59, to assemble this quilt. Note that using the patterns on page 66, you will appliqué a butterfly in the center of each block instead of an airplane. Using three strands of blue embroidery floss, backstitch two antennae and a wind swirl on each butterfly block (see backstitch diagram on page 36).

Wing
Cut 80.

Body
Cut 20.

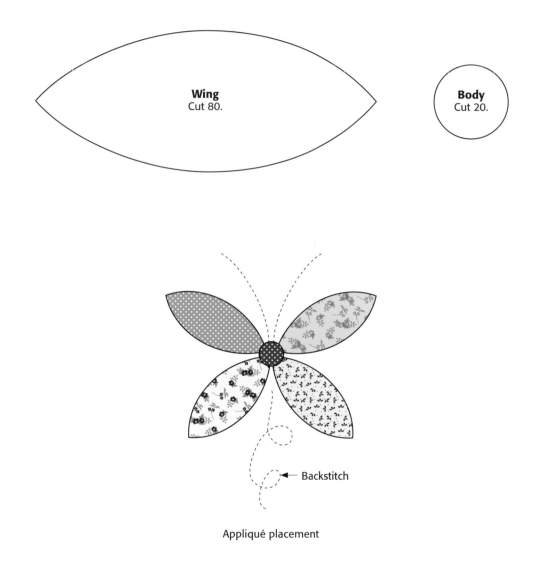

← Backstitch

Appliqué placement

QUILTMAKING BASICS

I HAVE INCLUDED tips and techniques used to make the projects in this book, and I hope they will benefit you in your quiltmaking. Please read this section carefully and refer to it as necessary.

FABRICS

I always use 100%-cotton fabrics. A good rule of thumb in selecting fabrics for a quilting project is to buy the best you can afford (although the most expensive fabric is not necessarily the best).

Sufficient yardage requirements are listed for all the projects in this book and are based on 42"-wide fabrics that provide at least 40" of usable fabric after prewashing and after selvages have been trimmed away. To vary the look of any design, use an assortment of scraps and purchase only those fabrics you need to complete the project you are making.

A good starting point for selecting fabric is to go with the color scheme for the eventual location of the quilt, such as your granddaughter's bedroom, for example. Choose a bolt of a multicolored print that will work in that color scheme. Select fabric colors using that print as a guide, and then put the bolt back on the shelf or perhaps use the print as the outer border of the quilt. After selecting all the fabrics, line them up, squint your eyes, and if two of the fabrics look the same, eliminate one of them.

I suggest prewashing all fabrics to test for colorfastness. This step also removes any excess dye that may be in the fabric. Iron the fabric before cutting to ensure accuracy. Another "quick" method I use to shrink fabric is to steam shrink it with a hot iron and a lot of steam. To achieve the vintage quilt look, don't prewash the fabric and use 100%-cotton batting. When the project is completed, throw it in the washer and dryer. Be sure to first test your fabrics for colorfastness when using this method.

SUPPLIES

Sewing machine: To machine piece, you will need a sewing machine that is in good working condition. If a ¼" foot is available for your machine, it is worth its weight in gold. A walking foot or darning foot makes machine quilting much easier.

Rotary-cutting tools: You will need a rotary cutter, cutting mat, and clear acrylic ruler. Rotary-cutting rulers are available in a variety of sizes: 6" x 24", 12" x 12", 6" x 6", and my favorite, 6" x 12".

Thread: Use a good-quality, all-purpose cotton thread. The stitching is always more even if the bobbin is wound from the same thread that is used on top. I use cream, white, and gray thread most often for piecing.

Needles: Always use a new needle for each new project. For machine piecing, a size 10/70 or 12/80 works best. For machine quilting, use a 12/80 or 14/90. For hand appliqué, choose a needle that will glide easily through the edges of the appliqué pieces. Size 10 (fine) to size 12 (very fine) needles are good choices.

Pins: My favorite pins are long with flat flower heads. These pins can be ironed over without leaving a trace on your fabric. Try different sizes; your preference may not be the same. Smaller, ½"- to ¾"-long sequin pins work best for appliqué.

Scissors: Use your best scissors only for cutting fabric. Use craft scissors to cut paper, fusible web, and template plastic. There are small, sharp scissors that are especially made for cutting threads.

Template plastic: Use clear or frosted plastic (available at quilt shops) to make durable, accurate templates.

Seam ripper: I use one every time I sew, and the sharper the seam ripper the better. I cut every fourth or fifth stitch, and then pull the one long thread from the other side.

Marking tools: A variety of tools are available to mark fabric when tracing around templates or marking quilting designs. Always test your marker on a scrap of fabric to make sure you can remove the marks easily.

ROTARY CUTTING

I love the speed and accuracy of this fabric-cutting method. I rely on quick and easy rotary cutting! All cutting measurements include standard ¼"-wide seam allowances. If you are unfamiliar with rotary cutting, read the brief introduction that follows. For more detailed information, see the book *The Quilter's Quick Reference Guide* by Candace Eisner Strick (Martingale & Company, 2004).

1. Fold the fabric in half, matching selvages and aligning the crosswise and lengthwise grains as much as possible. Place the folded edge closest to you on the cutting mat. Align a square ruler such as a Bias Square® along the folded edge of the fabric. Place a long, straight ruler to the left of the square ruler, just covering the uneven raw edges on the left side of the fabric. Remove the square ruler and cut along the right edge of the long ruler, rolling the rotary cutter away from you. Discard this strip. (Reverse this procedure if you are left-handed.)

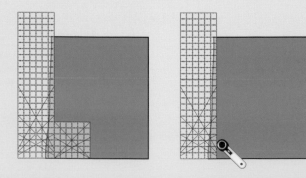

2. To cut strips, align the newly cut edge of the fabric with the ruler markings at the required width. For example, to cut a 3"-wide strip, place the 3" ruler mark on the edge of the fabric.

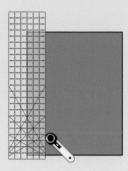

3. To cut squares, cut a strip of the specified width. Trim the selvage ends of the strips. Align the left edge of the strip with the correct ruler markings, the same measurement as the width of the strip. Cut the strip into squares until you have the number needed.

4. To cut half-square triangles, begin by cutting a square ⅞" larger than the finished size of the short side of the triangle. Then cut the square once diagonally, from corner to corner. Each square yields two half-square triangles. The short sides of each triangle are on the straight grain of the fabric.

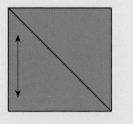
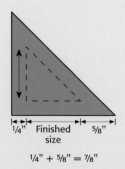

¼" Finished ⅝"
size

¼" + ⅝" = ⅞"

5. To cut quarter-square triangles, begin by cutting a square 1¼" larger than the finished size of the long side of the triangle. Then cut the square twice diagonally, from corner to corner. Each square yields four quarter-square triangles. The long side of each triangle is on the straight grain of the fabric.

5⁄8" | Finished size | 5⁄8"

5⁄8" + 5⁄8" = 1¼"

MACHINE PIECING

All of the quilts in this book are designed for the quickest piecing possible. Take the time to establish an exact ¼" seam allowance on any machine you use. Your machine may have a special quilting foot that measures exactly ¼" from the center needle position to the edge of the foot. This feature allows you to use the edge of the presser foot to guide the fabric for a perfect ¼"-wide seam allowance. If your machine doesn't have such a foot, create a seam guide by placing the edge of a piece of tape ¼" from the needle. By determining an exact ¼"-wide seam allowance for your piecing, your results will be more accurate.

Set your machine to sew 12 to 15 stitches per inch for normal piecing. Remember, if your stitches are too small and you need to rip them out, it becomes frustrating and time consuming. I always have a sharp seam ripper handy just in case. Likewise, stitches that are too large may not hold your quilt top together.

Accuracy is important when machine piecing, and matching points is not always easy. When matching seam lines while sewing pieces together, make sure the seam allowance on the bottom is pressed so that it moves easily over the feed dogs. Keep the top seam allowance pressed in the opposite direction. In other words, whenever possible, work with opposing seam allowances. This way the seams "lock" into position and line up exactly. Sometimes I find it necessary to change the pressing direction as the block is assembled to achieve opposing seams. Pin seam allowances in place if necessary.

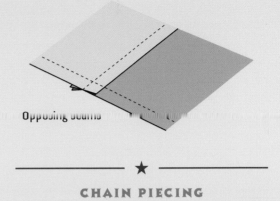

Opposing seams

★

CHAIN PIECING

When piecing by machine, you can save time and thread by using a stitching method called chain piecing. It's especially useful when making many identical units, like most of the quilt blocks in this book.

1. Stack pieces right sides together (pin if you like). Sew the first pair of pieces from cut edge to cut edge. Stop sewing at the end of the seam, but do not backstitch or clip the thread.

2. Feed the next pair of pieces under the presser foot, as close as possible to the first. Sew the seam and continue feeding pieces through the machine without cutting the threads in between the pairs.

3. When all the pairs are sewn, remove the chain from the machine and clip the threads between the pairs.

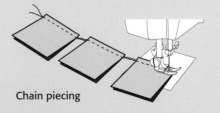

Chain piecing

PRESSING

The traditional rule in quiltmaking is to press seams to one side, toward the darker color wherever possible. First press the seams flat from the wrong side of the fabric (I call this a tack press); then press the seams in the desired direction from the right side. Press carefully to avoid distorting the shapes. Remember, there are always exceptions to the rule and it may be necessary to re-press as you assemble your blocks or rows.

APPLIQUÉ

I have included general instructions here for needle-turn, freezer-paper, and fusible appliqué. Feel free to use your favorite method regardless of the method described in the project. Just be sure to adapt the pattern pieces and project instructions as necessary. I have used the fusible-appliqué technique for all the appliqué projects in this book. All the pattern pieces have already been reversed for use with fusible web and can be traced "as is." If you choose to use another appliqué method, you may need to "reverse" the patterns in this book.

Making Templates

You will need to make a template of the appliqué pattern. I make my templates from clear plastic. Not only is the plastic more durable, but you can also see through the plastic when tracing or trying to fussy cut a particular image or design.

1. Place template plastic over each pattern piece and trace with a fine-line permanent marker. Do not add seam allowances.

2. Cut out the template just inside the drawn line. You need only one template for each different motif or shape.

3. Write the pattern name and grain-line arrow (if applicable) on the template. For fusible appliqué, you can trace the pattern onto the lightweight fusible web directly from the book.

Hand Appliqué

In traditional hand appliqué, the seam allowances are turned under before the appliqué is stitched to the background fabric. Two traditional methods for turning under the edges are needle-turn appliqué and freezer-paper appliqué. You can use either method to turn under the raw edges, and then use the traditional appliqué stitch or blind stitch to attach the shapes to your background fabric.

Freezer-Paper Appliqué

Freezer paper, which is coated on one side, is often used to stabilize the appliqué piece during the stitching process to help make nearly perfect appliqué shapes. It can also be used as a guide to turn under seam allowances before stitching.

1. Trace around the plastic template on the dull side (not the shiny side) of the freezer paper with a sharp pencil. You can also place the freezer paper, shiny side down, directly on top of the pattern and trace.

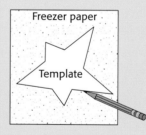

2. Cut out the traced design on the pencil line. Do not add seam allowances.

3. Iron the freezer-paper templates, shiny side down, to the wrong side of the appliqué fabric. Use a hot, dry iron and leave at least ¾" between pieces.

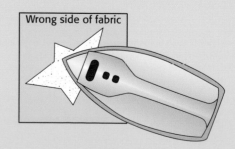

4. Cut around the fabric shapes, adding ¼" seam allowances around all the edges.

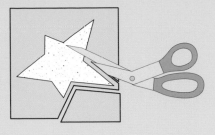

5. Turn the seam allowance over the freezer-paper edges and baste by hand, or use a fabric glue stick. Clip the inside points and fold the outside points as necessary.

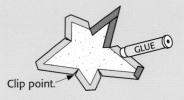

Clip point.

6. Pin or baste the design to the background fabric or block. Appliqué the design to the background with small stitches and matching thread. Letting the needle travel under the background fabric, parallel to the edge of the appliqué, bring it up about ⅛" away, along the pattern line. As you bring the needle up, pierce the edge of the appliqué piece, catching only a few threads of the folded edge. Refer to "Traditional Appliqué Stitch" that follows for additional details.

7. Remove any basting stitches. Cut a slit in the background fabric behind the appliqué and remove the freezer paper with tweezers. If you used glue stick, soak the piece in warm water for a few minutes before removing the freezer paper. Press.

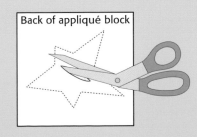

Back of appliqué block

Needle-Turn Appliqué

For needle-turn appliqué, cut out your shape ¼" larger than traced and clip around curves. Pin the shape in place to the background block and turn under the edges to the traced line as you appliqué the piece in place.

Traditional Appliqué Stitch

The traditional appliqué stitch or blind stitch is appropriate for sewing all appliqué shapes, including sharp points and curves.

1. Thread the needle with a single strand of thread, approximately 18" long, in a color that closely matches the color of your appliqué. Knot the thread tail.

2. Hide the knot by slipping the needle into the seam allowance from the wrong side of the appliqué piece, bringing it out on the fold line.

3. Work from right to left if you are right-handed or from left to right if you are left-handed. To make the first stitch, insert the needle into the background right next to where the needle came out of the appliqué fabric. Bring the needle up through the edge of the appliqué, about ⅛" from the first stitch. As you bring the needle up, pierce the basted edge of the appliqué piece, catching only a few threads.

4. Again, take a stitch into the background block right next to where the thread came up through the appliqué. Bring the needle up about ⅛" from the previous stitch, again catching the basted edge of the appliqué.

5. Give the thread a gentle pull and continue stitching.

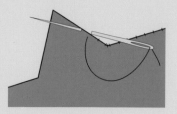

6. To end your stitching, pull the needle through to the wrong side. Behind the appliqué piece, take two small stitches, making knots by taking your needle through the loops. Check the right side to see if the thread tail shows through the background. If it does, take one more small stitch on the back to direct the tail of the thread under the appliqué fabric.

Fusible Appliqué

Using lightweight fusible web is a fast way to appliqué by machine. This method was used throughout the book. Use the patterns exactly as they appear.

Refer to the manufacturer's directions when applying fusible web to your fabrics; each brand is a little different, and pressing it too long may result in fusible web that doesn't stick well, although there is a product called Patch Attach (available at www.beaconcreates.com) that you can sprinkle on the back of your fabric to get your fusible web to fuse again if needed.

1. Trace or draw your shape on the paper side of the fusible web. Cut out the shape, leaving about a ¼" margin all around.

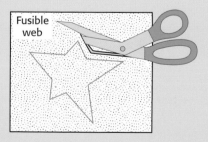

2. Fuse the shapes to the wrong side of your fabric. If your fabric is directional, take care to fuse the shapes accordingly.

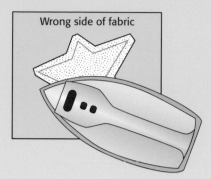

3. Cut out each shape exactly on the drawn line.

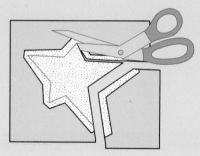

4. Remove the paper backing from the shape, position the shape on the background fabric, and fuse it in place with your iron. A product called Craft and Appliqué Sheet is very handy. This is a transparent, nonstick reusable sheet for pressing applications. You can layer your design on the sheet for perfect pattern placement, press all the layers together, remove the design when cooled, and position it onto the block as one piece. You can get these sheets online from Prairie Grove Peddler at www.prairiegrovepeddler.com.

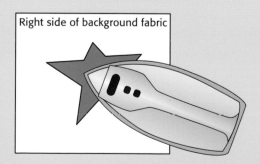

5. If desired, you can add decorative stitches by hand or machine around the edges of the fused appliqués. Commonly used stitches include satin stitches and blanket stitches. The projects in this book are edged with a machine blanket stitch. The hand blanket stitch is shown below.

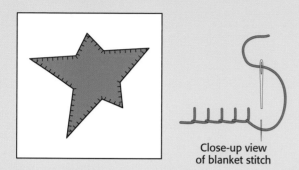

Close-up view
of blanket stitch

Alcohol wipes are handy to have around to remove any adhesive residue that might build up on your needle.

ASSEMBLING THE QUILT TOP

Squaring Up Blocks

After piecing your quilt blocks, take the time to square them up. Make sure the size is ½" larger than the finished size. If your blocks vary slightly in size, trim the larger blocks to match the size of the smallest block. Be sure to trim all four sides, otherwise, your block will be lopsided. If your blocks are not the correct finished size, other components of the quilt will need to be adjusted.

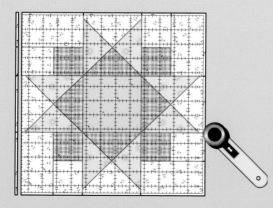

Straight Settings

1. Arrange the blocks as shown in the diagram provided with each quilt.

2. Sew the blocks together in horizontal or vertical rows according to the quilt instructions. Press the seams in opposite directions from row to row (unless otherwise directed).

3. Pin the rows together, being careful to match the block intersections from row to row. Sew the rows together and press the seams all in one direction.

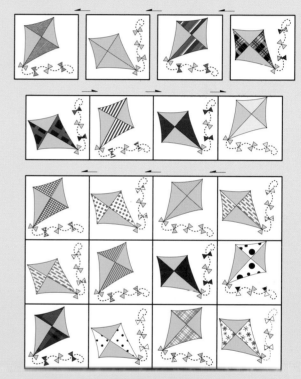

Straight-set quilt

Diagonal Settings

1. Arrange the blocks, side triangles, and corner triangles as shown in the diagram provided with each quilt. The side triangles and corner triangles will be larger than necessary and will be trimmed ¼" from the corner points of the blocks when the quilt top is completed.

2. Sew the blocks and side triangles together in diagonal rows; press the seams in the direction indicated by the project instructions.

3. Sew the rows together, matching seams. Sew corner triangles on last.

Diagonally set quilt

BORDERS

For best results, always measure your quilt before cutting or adding border strips. Quilts tend to "grow" on the outer edges as they get larger but remain the same through the center. Measure the quilt top through the center in both directions to determine how long to cut the border strips. This step ensures that your finished quilt will be as square as possible. Always ease the quilt top to fit the border strips.

Most of the quilts in this book call for plain border strips. The strips are cut along the crosswise grain and seamed where extra length is needed. Although the finished sizes of the quilts have been mathematically figured, I generally have not given any measurements for cutting your border-strip lengths. These measurements are determined once your quilt top is put together, as described in the butted-corner border method that follows.

1. Measure the length of the quilt top through the center. From the crosswise grain, cut two border strips to that measurement, piecing as necessary.

Mark the centers of the quilt edges and border strips. Pin the side borders to opposite sides of the quilt top, matching centers and ends and easing as necessary. Sew the border strips to the quilt top; press the seam allowances toward the borders.

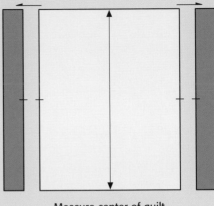

Measure center of quilt,
top to bottom. Mark centers.

2. Measure the width of the quilt top through the center, including the side borders just added. From the crosswise grain, cut two border strips to that measurement, piecing as necessary. Mark the centers of the quilt edges and the border strips. Pin the borders to the top and bottom edges of the quilt top, matching the center marks and ends and easing as necessary. Sew the border strips in place. Press the seams toward the border strips.

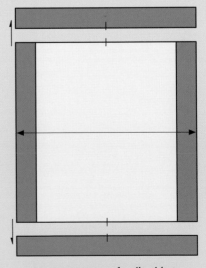

Measure center of quilt, side to
side, including border strips.
Mark centers.

PREPARING TO QUILT

Follow the directions in this section for marking, layering, and basting if you plan to quilt by hand or on your home sewing machine. If you plan to have a professional machine quilter quilt your project, check with that person before preparing your finished quilt top or backing in any way. Most of the quilts in this book were quilted by a long-arm machine quilter. To find a professional quilter in your area, check with your local quilt shop for referrals.

Marking Quilting Designs

After you complete the quilt top, give it a final pressing. Make sure that the seams all lie flat and are going in the correct direction. For quilting in the ditch (along the seam lines) or for free-motion random designs, marking is not necessary. Masking tape can be used on a basted quilt to mark straight lines. Tape only small sections at a time and remove the tape when you stop quilting for the day. If left on, sticky residue from the tape may be difficult to remove from your quilt top. If you plan to use detailed quilting patterns or complex designs, mark the quilt top before you baste the quilt layers together. Choose a marking tool that will be visible on your fabric and test it on scrap fabrics to be sure that the marks can be removed easily.

Layering and Basting the Quilt

The quilt backing and batting should be cut at least 4" to 6" longer and wider than the quilt top. For large quilts, it is usually necessary to sew two or three lengths of fabric together to make a backing that is large enough. Always trim away the selvages before piecing the lengths together. Press the seams open to make quilting easier by minimizing bulk. You might find it interesting to know that when I purchase fabric for a quilt, I often don't have a project in mind. I buy fabric in two- or three-yard pieces; therefore I have a lot of excess fabric hanging around. If you could see the backs of my quilts, you would see that most, but not all, are pieced together with different large pieces of fabric or scraps from the quilt top. This ensures that no fabric goes to waste and I can buy more. Note that the materials list for each project gives the amount of fabric necessary to make a backing from one fabric.

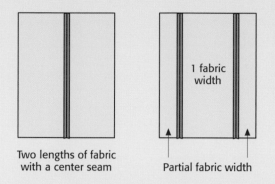

Two lengths of fabric with a center seam

1 fabric width

Partial fabric width

Batting comes packaged in standard bed sizes, or it can be purchased by the yard in many different weights or thicknesses. A thinner batting is best if you intend to quilt by hand or machine, and the quilt will have a nicer drape. I recommend a product made exclusively for machine quilters by Fairfield Company called Machine 60/40 Blend. The special blend makes it softer to touch, the needle glides more smoothly, the quilt hangs flat, and my favorite thing is that it prevents creases from forming when the quilt is folded.

1. Spread the backing wrong side up on a flat, clean surface. Anchor it with pins or masking tape. Be careful not to stretch the backing out of shape.

2. Spread the batting over the backing, smoothing wrinkles from the center out.

3. Center the pressed quilt top on top of the batting. Again, smooth wrinkles from the center out, making sure the quilt-top edges are parallel to the edges of the backing.

4. Starting in the center, baste with needle and thread and work diagonally to each corner. Then baste a grid of horizontal and vertical lines 6" to 8" apart.

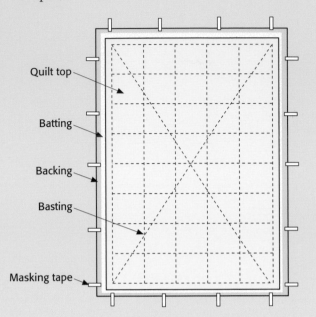

Quilt top
Batting
Backing
Basting
Masking tape

NOTE: *For machine quilting, you may baste the layers with #2 rustproof safety pins. Place the pins about 6" to 8" apart and remove them as you go.*

MACHINE QUILTING

Machine quilting is suitable for all types of quilts. With machine quilting, you can quickly complete quilts and move on to the next project. Marking the quilting design is optional. In most cases, these quilts lend themselves to straight-line quilting, or free-motion quilting in a random pattern. However, if you choose to do what I do, simply send the quilt top and backing to a professional quilter and let her choose the quilting pattern and the batting she thinks is appropriate.

For straight-line quilting, it is extremely helpful to have a walking foot to help feed the quilt layers through the machine without shifting or puckering. Some machines have a built-in walking foot; most machines require a separate attachment. To stitch in the ditch, you quilt on the seam lines between the pieces. Mark the lines to follow or use masking tape for other straight-line quilting designs. Be sure to remove any masking tape when you finish quilting each day, because it may leave a residue if left on the quilt too long.

Walking foot

For free-motion quilting, you need a darning foot and the ability to drop or cover the feed dogs on your machine. Consult your sewing-machine instruction manual if you need help. With free-motion quilting, you guide the fabric in the direction of the design rather than turning the fabric under the needle. With a little practice you can become an expert in no time, and you can quilt curves and loops of any size and shape.

Darning foot

HAND QUILTING

Hand quilting is the time-honored method of holding the layers of a quilt together, but it does take longer than machine quilting. To quilt by hand, use a short, sturdy needle called a Between. Start with a size 8 and gradually work toward using smaller needles (the higher the number, the smaller the needle). You will also need a thimble for your middle finger, quilting thread (especially made for hand quilting), and a hoop or frame to hold the quilt sandwich for stitching.

1. Thread your needle with a length of quilting thread about 18" long. Make a small knot in one end. Insert the needle into the top layer and batting of the quilt about ½" from where you want to begin stitching. Pull the needle out at the point where stitching will begin and gently pull the thread until the knot pops through the fabric and into the batting.

2. Using your thimble to control the needle, insert the needle vertically into the quilt. Place your other hand underneath the quilt so that you can feel the needle point with the top of your finger when the needle is through the layers. Rock the needle back up through the layers and down again until you have three or four stitches on the needle. Pull the needle through and repeat the stitching process.

3. To end a line of quilting, make a small knot close to the last stitch; then make a backstitch and slide the needle through the batting about ½" away. Bring the needle up and gently pull on the thread until the knot pops into the batting. Snip the thread at the quilt's surface.

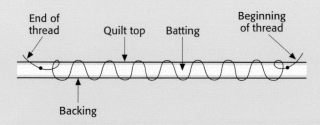

FINISHING

Follow these simple steps for adding a hanging sleeve (optional), binding, and a label.

Hanging Sleeve

If your quilt is going to be displayed on a wall, you may want to add a permanent hanging sleeve. A hanging sleeve creates a secure way to insert a rod and will support the quilt evenly. The addition of a hanging sleeve makes it simple to change the look of a room because you can easily remove a quilt from the rod and replace it with another from your quilt collection. However, if the quilt is very small, I use several map pins across the top and on each corner to hang it on a wall rather than a hanging sleeve and rod. A map pin has a regular-size round pin head and a ⅜" pin.

1. From the leftover quilt backing fabric, cut a strip 6" to 8" wide and 1" shorter than the width of your quilt. Fold the ends under ½", and then ½" again to make a hem. Stitch the hems in place.

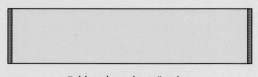

Fold ends under ½" twice.

2. Fold the fabric strip in half lengthwise, wrong sides together, and baste the raw edges to the top of the quilt back. The top edge of the sleeve will be secured when the binding is sewn on the quilt.

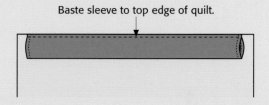

Baste sleeve to top edge of quilt.

3. After the binding has been attached, finish the sleeve by blindstitching the bottom of the sleeve in place. Before sewing the bottom edge in place, push the sleeve up just a bit to provide a little excess fabric for the hanging rod; this will keep the rod from putting strain on the quilt.

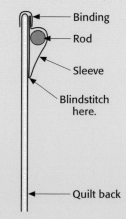

Binding

I prefer French double-fold binding. All the bindings for the quilts in this book were cut 2½" wide across the width of fabric and then pieced. You will need enough strips to go around the perimeter of the quilt, plus 10" for seams and finishing the corners. You'll notice that some of the quilts have scrappy bindings. These bindings were made using strips cut from the quilt-top fabrics. There are no specific rules when cutting these strips; they can range in length from 8" to 20" long. They are then sewn together randomly, end to end.

Below are instructions for the lapped-corner method of attaching binding. Use a walking foot, if you have one, when sewing the binding to the quilt. It helps to feed all the layers through the machine evenly.

1. Trim the batting and backing even with the quilt top. Add a hanging sleeve, if desired, before adding the binding (see "Hanging Sleeve" on page 77).

2. Join the binding strips to make one long strip. Sew the strips right sides together at right angles, stitching across the corner as shown. Trim the seam to ¼" and press open.

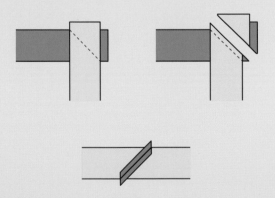

3. Fold the binding strip in half lengthwise, wrong sides together, and press.

4. Measure the quilt top vertically through the center and cut two strips of binding to this length for side bindings. Use a ¼" seam allowance to stitch the binding to the sides of the quilt, keeping the raw edges of the binding even with the trimmed edges of quilt.

5. Fold the binding over the edges of the quilt to the back, with the folded edge covering the row of machine stitching. Blindstitch the binding in place.

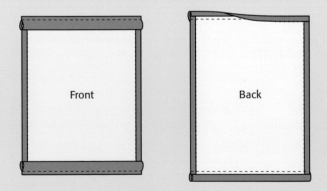

Match raw edges.

6. Measure the quilt top horizontally through the center and cut two strips of binding to this measurement, plus 1". Fold under ½" on each end of the binding and press. Stitch the binding to the top and bottom of the quilt, keeping the raw edges even with the quilt-top edges. Fold the binding to the back and finish the same as the side bindings. Slipstitch the ends closed.

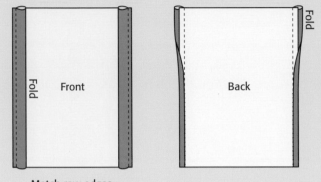

Signing Your Quilt

Please be sure to sign and date your quilts by adding a label to the back. It is important to include the name of the quilt, your name, the quilter's name (if different from you), your city and state, the date, and the intended recipient, if desired. By documenting your quilt with something as simple as a label, future generations will be able to learn a little bit of its history.

Stabilize your label fabric by ironing a piece of freezer paper to the wrong side. Use a fine-tipped, permanent fabric pen to record the information on the fabric and remove the freezer paper. Attach it to the back of the quilt with small stitches, or blanket stitch it in place. You may also type, print, or embroider your information on the fabric before sewing it to the back of your quilt. Another idea is to make an extra block, using a light-colored fabric as one of the larger pieces, for your label.

Red 'n' Hot

by Retta Warehime
Kennewick, WA 2005
51" x 51"
Made for Terry Layden

ABOUT THE AUTHOR

RETTA WAREHIME lives with her husband, Dan, and son, Gregg, in Kennewick, Washington. Her three daughters and their children are all nearby in the Tri-Cities area.

She has been designing quilts for over 20 years, continues to be active in the fabric industry, and currently serves on a quilting advisory board. Most recently she has been designing quilts for Web sites, ghostwriting and sewing for other designers, and teaching on cruise ships, which she says is "great fun!" She recently went on a cruise to Alaska with her mother, Marlene, and her sister Kathy—their first trip together.

Retta loves gardening, boating, hockey games, shopping, coffee, and travel. Mostly she loves doing all of those things with friends and family.